Twayne's United States Authors Series

Sylvia E. Bowman, *Editor*

INDIANA UNIVERSITY

George Cabot Lodge

TUSAS 264

George Cabot Lodge

GEORGE CABOT LODGE

By JOHN W. CROWLEY

Syracuse University

TWAYNE PUBLISHERS

A DIVISION OF G. K. HALL & CO., BOSTON

Library of Congress Cataloging in Publication Data

Crowley, John William, 1945–
  George Cabot Lodge.

  (Twayne's United States authors series; TUSAS
264)
  Bibliography: p. 139–43.
  Includes index.
  1. Lodge, George Cabot, 1873–1909.
PS2249.L34Z6   811'.4   [B]   75-44429
ISBN 0-8057-7165-4

For Matthew and Anne

Contents

About the Author

John W. Crowley is Associate Professor of English at Syracuse University where he has taught since 1970. Holder of a B. A. degree from Yale University and a Ph. D. from Indiana University, Professor Crowley has published numerous articles on American writers. He has also edited *George Cabot Lodge: Selected Fiction and Verse* and *A Foregone Conclusion* for A Selected Edition of W. D. Howells. Professor Crowley is currently engaged in work on fiction of and about New England.

Preface

Although George Cabot Lodge never enjoyed a major reputation in his lifetime, his six volumes of poetry and verse-drama elicited favorable reviews in some quarters and impressed a circle of friends and acquaintances that included Henry and Brooks Adams, Bernard Berenson, Henry James, Theodore Roosevelt, and Edith Wharton. It was rare for books of poetry to sell more than a few hundred copies in the period of Lodge's publication (1898–1909), and Lodge's books were no exceptions. But he was well enough respected as a writer to be elected to the National Institute of Arts and Letters in 1908.

This book, the first extended study of Lodge since 1911, rests on two premises: that, if George Cabot Lodge was not a great author, he was at least a respectable minor author; and that his career is symptomatic of the stresses borne by many other modern American writers. Because Lodge's life and work are so inextricably linked, I have fitted my discussion of each of his volumes into a biographical context. Since Lodge's work is unfamiliar to most readers, and since many of his letters have never before been published, I have quoted liberally from both.

After considering Lodge's family background, formative influences on his life, and his Harvard years in Chapter 1, I treat each of his volumes in chronological order. Chapter 2 views *The Song of the Wave and Other Poems* from the perspective of "The Genteel Tradition." In Chapter 3, I define what Lodge meant by Conservative Christian Anarchism and apply this definition to *Poems (1899–1902)* and to his extant novels, "Mediocracy" and "The Genius of the Commonplace." Chapter 4 discusses *Cain: A Drama* as part of an American revival of mythic verse-drama, and relates *The Great Adventure* to the death of Trumbull Stickney and to Lodge's editing of Stickney's work. Chapters 5 and 6 trace the culmination of Lodge's transcendental optimism in *Herakles* and the isolation of his last years. Chapter 7 examines the history of Lodge's literary reputation and the relationship of his career to the prevailing literary-historical interpretation of his era as one stifling to writers.

Brief portions of Chapters 1, 3, and 7 have appeared in different forms respectively in *Essex Institute Historical Collections, Walt Whitman Review,* and *New England Quarterly.*

JOHN W. CROWLEY

Syracuse University

Acknowledgments

I am grateful to the three children of George Cabot Lodge— Helena, Baroness de Streel, John Davis Lodge, and Henry Cabot Lodge—without whose extraordinary cooperation and encouragement this project would have been impossible.

I am especially indebted to Edwin H. Cady, whose unflagging interest sustained and inspired me throughout the first phase of this book, and to Stephen T. Riley and John D. Cushing and the staff of the Massachusetts Historical Society.

I have quoted many unpublished letters in this book with the permission of these literary executors: James B. Ames (for Henry Adams and Brooks Adams), Frederick J. Fawcett (for William Vaughn Moody), Valentine M. Gammell (for Langdon Mitchell and S. Weir Mitchell), Julian Trevelyan (for Robert Calverley Trevelyan), and Armitage Watkins (for Edith Wharton). Furthermore, the following libraries have graciously granted me permission to publish letters in their collections: the Massachusetts Historical Society, Columbia University Library, Yale University Library, Princeton University Library.

I also wish to thank several persons, academic and otherwise, who helped me to complete this book: Seán Haldane and the late Bernhard Knollenberg, who gave the book a careful and critical reading at an earlier stage; R. W. B. Lewis, who helped me gain access to Edith Wharton's papers; Jay Martin, who led me to work on Lodge in the first place; and Elwood Myers, who captained our voyage to Tuckernuck Island.

Finally, Sheila Crowley contributed substantially and selflessly to this book from its beginning.

J. W. C.

Chronology

1873   George Cabot Lodge born October 10 to Anna Cabot Mills Lodge and Henry Cabot Lodge at Nahant, Massachusetts.

1886   Henry Cabot Lodge elected to Congress.

1887   Lodge family moves from Boston to Washington, D.C.

1891   George Cabot Lodge enters Harvard College.

1895   Publishes first poem in the *Harvard Monthly*; graduates from Harvard; studies at the Sorbonne.

1896   Studies in Paris.

1897   Studies in Berlin; becomes private secretary to his father.

1898   Serves in Spanish-American War; publishes *The Song of the Wave and Other Poems*.

1899   Writes several unpublished plays and novels.

1900   Marries Elizabeth Freylinghuysen Davis (August 18); honeymoons in Paris.

1901   In Paris, writes "Mediocracy" and unpublished versedramas; returns to Washington.

1902   Writes "The Genius of the Commonplace"; publishes *Poems (1899–1902)*; birth of first son, Henry Cabot Lodge, Jr.

1903   Birth of second son, John Davis Lodge.

1904   Publishes *Cain: A Drama*; Trumbull Stickney dies (October 11).

1905   Edits, with John Ellerton Lodge and William Vaughn Moody, *The Poems of Trumbull Stickney*; publishes *The Great Adventure*; birth of daughter, Helena Lodge.

1906   Delivers the Phi Beta Kappa poem at Harvard.

1907   Develops heart trouble.

1908   Elected to National Institute of Arts and Letters; publishes *Herakles*.

1909   Dies on Tuckernuck Island, Massachusetts, August 21. *The Soul's Inheritance and Other Poems* published posthumously.

1911 *Poems and Dramas of George Cabot Lodge* and Henry Adams's *Life of George Cabot Lodge* published.

1976 "The Genius of the Commonplace" published in *George Cabot Lodge: Selected Fiction and Verse.*

CHAPTER 1

The Education of George Cabot Lodge

"PARENTAGE and ancestry are no longer in biography merely a means of definition," Henry Cabot Lodge wrote in 1916. "Heredity is now not only an inseparable but an indispensable part of the task of the biographer. . . . We no longer smile at Dr. Holmes' remark that a man's education should begin one hundred and fifty years before his birth, for the saying involves a great scientific truth."[1] Lodge implied that the character of a man of family would inevitably be molded by consciousness of family. Family consciousness was not peculiar to New England in the nineteenth century; yet, as Nathaniel Hawthorne and others had warned, to the New England mind the family past often became a curse, a source of guilt and of disorientation from the present. In part, such was the case of George Cabot Lodge, who could trace his American ancestry well beyond one hundred and fifty years—in fact, directly to John Howland, who arrived on the *Mayflower*, and to Francis Higginson, the first minister of the Massachusetts Bay Colony.

I The Family Tradition

Early in the eighteenth century, Elizabeth Higginson, a direct descendant of Francis Higginson, married Joseph Cabot, whose father, John, had emigrated from the Isle of Jersey to Salem in 1699. John Cabot had wedded a Salem merchant's daughter and amassed a fortune in the rum and molasses trade. Two of his sons, Joseph and Francis, inherited his mercantile shrewdness with his business; as privateers during the French and Indian War, the Cabot brothers multiplied their father's wealth. It was Joseph Cabot's seventh son George, however, who became the "merchant prince" of the family.

Expelled from Harvard for disciplinary reasons, George Cabot was sent to sea to learn the family business. Before the American Revolution, George Cabot earned a reputation as an aggressive

15

trader; when war broke out, he exploited it as a privateer. Rich before the age of thirty, Cabot entered politics after the revolution, first as a founder of the North Shore Essex Junto and later as United States senator from Massachusetts. Cabot strongly endorsed Alexander Hamilton's economic policies; and, through associations with Hamilton, George Washington, John Adams, and Fisher Ames, he influenced the policies of the Federalist party. When the power of the Federalists waned, George Cabot feared the subjugation of New England interests to those of the South and West. His consequent involvement in the Hartford Convention of 1814 elicited an angry reproach from his old ally Adams: "He wants to be president of New England, sir."[2]

The putative president of New England had once entertained President Washington at his Beverly mansion, an event that Cabot's son Henry (then seven) witnessed hidden beneath the sidetable and that Henry Cabot lived to relate to his grandson and namesake Henry Cabot Lodge. Henry Cabot apparently lacked the family instinct for trade; after a brief career in the insurance business, he retired to a gentleman's life in Boston. In 1842, Henry Cabot's daughter Anna married John Ellerton Lodge, the son of an English merchant, Giles Lodge, who had fled Santo Domingo for Boston in 1791. John Ellerton Lodge compounded his father's and his wife's wealth through success in the China Trade. Their only son Henry Cabot Lodge was assured at his birth in 1850 not only of social prominence but of financial independence.

In his autobiography, Henry Cabot Lodge noted, "As I conclude this brief outline of my New England ancestry I am struck by the lack of what is usually conspicuous in such pedigrees—the clerical strain. Except for Francis Higginson . . . I find on both sides merchants and sailors, sea-captains and soldiers, men of action and men in business and in public life, but no clergymen. They seem on both sides likewise to have been, as a rule, hardy, active, and successful, taking part in the life of their time, and filling a place in the world, whether large or small, by work and energy."[3]

Implicit in Lodge's observation that his family lacked the "clerical strain" was the realization that his ancestors did not qualify as members of the "Brahmin caste." As defined by Oliver Wendell Holmes, the "Brahmin caste of New England" comprised a select number of families whose members distinguished themselves generation after generation as men of thought rather than of action. According to Holmes, this "harmless, inoffensive, untitled aristocracy" bred a race of scholars in which aptitude for learning was congenital. The Brahmin caste "exchanged a certain portion of its animal vigor for its new instincts." In contrast to an average yeoman, the typical Brahmin exhibited emaciation or even femininity: "His face is smooth, and apt to be pallid,—his features are regular and of a certain delicacy,—his eye is bright and quick,—his lips play over the thought he utters as a pianist's fingers dance over their music,—and his whole air, though it may be timid, and even awkward, has nothing clownish."[4] The hardy Cabots and Lodges, whose faces were etched by the sea, were men accustomed to decisive action; and they shared neither the pallor nor the speculative temper of the Brahmins.

Rather, in Cleveland Amory's phrase, they were "Proper Bostonians," families whose social position resulted not so much from their *Mayflower* ancestry or their intellectual distinction as from their commercial success. Behind every "First Family" in Boston, Amory discerns a nineteenth-century "merchant prince" whose business acumen ensured affluence for the future generations of the family: "Whether in shipping, in railroading, in textiles, in mining, or in banking, he [the merchant prince] is the stout trunk of almost every First Family tree. . . . There is scarcely a Family that does not owe its position in the city's Society to the money he made and saved and left in the spendthrift-proof trusts for them."[5] Henry Cabot Lodge became the first of his family to break entirely with its mercantile tradition; and he recognized his indebtedness for the opportunity to his merchant great-grandfather George Cabot, after whom he named his first son, George Cabot Lodge, who was born on October 10, 1873. Dubbed "*Ba*-by" by his sister Constance, George Cabot Lodge for the rest of his life was known as "Bay."

II   *Formative Influences*

Little is known about Bay Lodge's childhood. His life centered on his family, and his closest companion was his younger brother, John Ellerton Lodge. His education followed the usual "classical" curriculum, first at the Noble School in Boston and, after his father went to Congress, at the Emerson Institute in Washington. Even as a child, Lodge demonstrated the abstract habit of mind that later marked his poetry. A dreamer by temperament, Lodge often drifted in the classroom. His teacher at Emerson found him "very capable, but lazy and consequently inaccurate."[6]

Lodge's mother, Anna Cabot Mills Lodge, was a charming, intelligent, well-read woman who, despite her self-effacing manner, exerted a powerful influence on both her husband's and her son's careers. Lodge, always very close to his mother, characteristically turned to her in times of stress. But equally formative influences on his life were the three men he loved best: his father, and his father's closest friends, William Sturgis Bigelow and Theodore Roosevelt. The careers of these three presented to young Lodge widely varying examples to follow.

Henry Cabot Lodge's political success ultimately eclipsed his literary achievement, but the Brahmin life tempted Lodge as a young man. As Owen Wister noted, "He could easily, as well as Holmes or Adams, have made his name as a writer, which he had begun to do. He left an excellent literary beginning for the life of action."[7] While at Harvard, Henry Cabot Lodge decided that a career "which combined that of the public man and of the man of letters, was the most enviable which could be imagined."[8] In other words, Lodge projected for himself a life combining the best Proper Bostonian and Brahmin elements. Encouraged by Henry Adams to pursue a "historico-literary" career in the tradition of John Lothrop Motley, Francis Parkman, George Bancroft, and William Hickling Prescott, Lodge after graduation became Adams's assistant on the *North American Review*.

During the same period, Lodge completed his law degree (1874) and finished his doctoral dissertation under Adams (published in 1876 in *Essays in Anglo-Saxon Law*). In the fall of 1876, President Charles W. Eliot appointed him to teach colonial American history at Harvard. From his course lectures, Lodge prepared a series of Lowell Institute Lectures, published in 1881 as *A Short History of the English Colonies in America*. In 1878, he published *The Life and Letters of George Cabot*. The *History* and *George Cabot* earned Lodge a minor literary reputation, and his articles were readily accepted by the *Nation* and the *Atlantic Monthly*. After resigning from Harvard (because of a salary dispute with Eliot) and from the *North American Review*, Lodge joined John T. Morse as co-editor of the *International Review*. Subsequently, Lodge collaborated with Morse on the American Statesmen Series, writing biographies of Washington, Alexander Hamilton, and Daniel Webster.

During the 1870s, Lodge entered local Republican politics; he began in 1879 the first of several terms in the lower house of the Massachusetts General Court. In 1882 he ran unsuccessfully for state senator. In 1884 Lodge weathered the first crisis of his political career; although he opposed the candidacy of James G. Blaine at the Republican convention, Lodge subsequently supported the presidential nomination of Blaine in the face of strong opposition from his New England colleagues. Lodge's party loyalty resulted in his own nomination for Congress; after winning the 1886 election, he served several terms as congressman from the North Shore district and, after 1893, as United States senator until his death in 1924. Even as his commitment to politics deepened, Lodge continued to be a prolific writer of historical articles and books. He read voraciously all his life; and, although he particularly admired the authors who had befriended him during his tenure on the *North American Review*—Holmes, Henry Wadsworth Longfellow, James Russell Lowell, Ralph Waldo Emerson, John Greenleaf Whittier, W. D. Howells, Mark Twain, and Thomas Bailey Aldrich—Lodge read and corresponded with writers of his own and his son's generations. The literary side of Henry Cabot Lodge's career explains in part his enthusiasm for his son's poetic calling. Once he was convinced that Bay had both the desire and the talent to write poetry, Lodge never failed to encourage this choice of career. Not only did he support his son and subsidize all his books, he crusaded after Bay's death to keep his literary reputation alive. In his own life Henry Cabot Lodge struck a compromise between a "historico-literary" career and the family tradition of "taking part in the life of [the] time, and filling a place in the world." To the extent that Lodge was a Brahmin *manqué*, George Cabot Lodge as a poet represented a fulfillment and vindication of his father's Brahmin aspirations.

The Brahmin life in a purer, if more decadent, form was represented to George Cabot Lodge by William Sturgis Bigelow, his father's oldest friend. Bigelow's father and grandfather had been distinguished physicians at the Harvard Medical School, and Bigelow was coerced into following in their footsteps. After dutifully obtaining a medical degree and practicing for two years as a surgeon in Boston, Bigelow abandoned medicine altogether. In 1881, to escape his father and his profession, Bigelow accompanied art historian Edward S. Morse to Japan in search of art treasures. Bigelow remained eight years, and amassed an exquisite collection that now is in the Boston Museum of Fine Arts. With Ernest Fenollosa, another protégé of Morse, Bigelow studied Japanese culture and became a convert to Northern Buddhism.

After returning to Boston in 1889, Bigelow generated among his friends a cultish interest in Buddhism. On George Cabot Lodge, at the impressionable age of fifteen when Bigelow returned, Bigelow's Eastern philosophy had a profounder effect. Bigelow, who never married, regarded Bay Lodge as a son, and Lodge confided in him throughout his life. The impact of Bigelow's Buddhism on Lodge's poetry, although evident in the early volumes, became more apparent in verse-dramas in which Lodge attempted to synthesize his understanding of Buddhism with the philosophies of Arthur Schopenhauer and Friedrich Nietzsche.

Bigelow's unorthodox ideas and his enigmatic manner aroused distrust in some who knew him. Edith Wharton, who deplored his influence over Lodge, recalled Bigelow as a man "whose erudition so far exceeded his mental capacity."[9] Van Wyck Brooks, who suggested that Bigelow was the model for Dr. Peter Alden in Santayana's *The Last Puritan*, suspected fraudulence in his spiritualism. "Received into Buddhism, he 'emanated a peaceful radiance,' one of his later friends said, 'mingled with a faint fragrance of toilet water,' but this was after he returned to Boston, full of Buddhist lore, believing he had been aware of his former incarnations. He preferred, this friend said, an Asiatic religion while wearing beautiful Charvet neckties and handsome English clothes, and, a bearded mystic and epicure, he lived, in fastidious luxury, with the rarest wines and exquisite food and every kind of exotic delicacy."[10] When Bigelow died, his religion embarrassed his family; he had requested cremation—in his oriental robes. With Bishop William Lawrence officiating, Bigelow had an incongruous Episcopalian funeral; but only half his ashes were buried in Mount Auburn Cemetery, the final resting place of eminent Bostonians that Bigelow's grandfather had helped to establish. The other half were carried to Japan and placed beside Fenollosa's in a Buddhist temple on the shores of Lake Biwa.

In life as in death, only half of Bigelow belonged to Boston, and that half did so with his reluctance. As a friend described him, "In a mediaeval setting he might have been a mediaeval saint, or a mystic, or might even have founded an enduring order; but New England and the present day breeds saints of another type."[11] It hardly seems a coincidence that Cecil Spring Rice in 1909 had written a nearly identical sentence to characterize George Cabot Lodge: "I think he was the sort of stuff that in the middle ages would have made a great saint or a great heresiarch—I dare say we have no use

for such people now."[12] Temperamentally, neither Bigelow nor
Lodge was suited to Boston. Because Boston to some extent ostracized them for eccentricity, Bigelow and Lodge withdrew often
to a sanctuary on Tuckernuck Island.

On Tuckernuck, a small island off the western coast of Nantucket,
Bigelow maintained a luxurious gentlemen's retreat where his
friends could join him or retire singly during the summer. Women
were forbidden at Tuckernuck; and the men, attended by a staff of
servants, feasted and relaxed in an atmosphere that to some seemed
Edenic. Charles Warren Stoddard, after his first visit there, compared life on Tuckernuck to "the Golden Age of Greece": "Sometimes I look up from my book and my eye rests upon a vista of
enchanting loveliness. Sea and sky in harmonious conjunction; the
clouds emphasizing every beauty; the distant sails like pearls set in
lapis lazuli. Then I say to myself: 'I must look always; I must not lose
one moment of this, for it is a glimpse of Paradise.' " Remote from
the pressures of life on the mainland, Tuckernuck drugged its vis-
itors with an eerie sense of timelessness. As Stoddard described it,
"The days are undistinguished; there are night and day, a fair day, a
foul day, and moonlight—that is all."[13] The island also seemed to
dissolve a sense of history and personal identity. Existence on Tuckernuck approximated, perhaps, the state of Nirvana; and this
spiritual dimension informed Lodge's sonnet about the island:

> I am content to live the patient day:
>   The wind sea-laden loiters to the land
>   And on the glittering gold of naked sand
>   The eternity of blue sea pales to spray.
> In such a world we have no need to pray;
>   The holy voices of the sea and air
>   Are sacramental, like a mighty prayer
>   In which the earth had dreamed its tears away.
> We row across the water's fluent gold
>   And age seems blessed, for the world is old,
>   Softly we take from Nature's open palm
> The dower of the sunset and the sky,
>   And dream an Eastern dream, starred by the cry
>   Of sea-birds homing through the mighty calm.[14]

Lodge, who spent nearly every summer on Tuckernuck, was tempted by the dream of an Eastern dream, or by Bigelow's life of with-

drawal. However, the life of immersion, personified by his father and even more by Theodore Roosevelt, exerted an equally strong attraction over Lodge as a young man.

In 1905, President Roosevelt finally yielded to Bigelow's invitations and arrived on Tuckernuck Island. When his boat landed, Roosevelt must have known at a glance that Tuckernuck offered neither the bustle of civilization nor the challenge of the wilderness as he had known it in the Dakota Bad Lands. His entourage straining to keep pace, Roosevelt rambled down the beach to the house. In less than twenty-four hours, bored and satisfied that he had exhausted the resources of the island, Roosevelt returned to the mainland. His predictable immunity to Tuckernuck illustrates dramatically the divergence of his life from Bigelow's.

At about the same time that he first met Henry Cabot Lodge in 1883, Theodore Roosevelt bought an interest in two cattle ranches near Medora in the Dakota Territory; and, until the harsh winter of 1886–87 killed his stock, Roosevelt immersed himself in the rugged life of the prairie. At first the butt of endless jokes about his spectacles and his high-flown manner of speech, Roosevelt vied with the cowboys at their own skills and gradually won their respect. In retrospect, life in the Bad Lands assumed epic proportions: "It was still the Wild West in those days, the Far West, the West of Owen Wister's stories and Frederick Remington's drawings, the West of the Indian and the buffalo-hunter, the soldier and the cowpuncher. . . . We knew toil and hardship and hunger and thirst; and we saw men die violent deaths as they worked among the horses and cattle, or fought in evil feuds with one another; but we felt the beat of hardy life in our veins, and ours was the glory of work and the joy of living." Whereas Tuckernuck provided a life of luxurious idleness in which physical exertion never passed beyond sports, the "Wild West" reduced life to an elemental confrontation of man with unyielding nature and strained the limits of man's courage and endurance. It was essentially a life of action, often violent action, which left no time for contemplation. "It taught a man self-reliance, hardihood, and the value of instant decision—in short, the virtues that ought to come from life in the open country."[15] To Roosevelt, life on Tuckernuck must have seemed a decadent perversion of life in the open country.

Roosevelt cast himself in the role of prophet to an America made flabby, physically and morally, by commercial success: "I wish to preach, not the doctrine of ignoble ease, but the doctrine of the strenuous life, the life of toil and effort, of labor and strife; to preach that highest form of success which comes, not to the man who desires mere easy peace, but to the man who does not shrink from danger, from hardship, or from bitter toil, and who out of these wins the splendid ultimate triumph."[16] Throughout his long friendship with George Cabot Lodge, Roosevelt proselytized for a life of manly action; and he personally supervised Lodge's initiation into the strenuous life by inviting him to Dakota for a hunting trip in the fall of 1890.

III   A Boston Aesthete

Almost everyone who recorded an impression of George Cabot Lodge remarked his combination of dashingly handsome appearance with a magnetic personality. A picture-book child with flowing blond curls, Lodge matured into a strapping man, well over six feet tall, who seemed almost to be the incarnation of his Promethean heroes. The daughter of his friend Langdon Mitchell recalled her childish intoxication with him: "I remember Bay staying with us in Cornish, N.H., & the impression he made on me—the high shoulders, the blue eyes, the laughing face & the quick, graceful movements. I was a child, but felt his fascination."[17] So did Edith Wharton, who found it impossible to distinguish her reaction to his poetry from her remembrance of him as a man: "The first impression he made was of a joyous physical life. His sweet smile, his easy strength, his deep eyes full of laughter and visions—these struck one even before his look of intellectual power. I have seldom seen any one in whom the natural man was so wholesomely blent with the reflecting intelligence; and it was not the least of his charms that he sent such stout roots into the earth, and had such a hearty love for all he drew from it."[18]

Henry Adams, who would have a great influence on him, believed that the George Cabot Lodge who "identified himself with the energies of nature" was the true man. According to Adams, the development of Lodge's "reflecting intelligence" in response to the expectations of his society failed to alter his elemental simplicity: "Throughout life, the more widely his character spread in circumference, the more simply he thought, and even when trying to grow complex,—as was inevitable since it was to grow in Boston,—the mind itself was never complex, and the complexities merely gathered on it, as something outside, like the seaweeds gathering and swaying about the rocks."[19]

Lodge's life and work were shaped by a cluster of related tensions—between the "reflecting intelligence" and the "natural man," between complexity and simplicity, between the life of action and the life of thought, and ultimately between immersion in the multiplicity of modern life and withdrawal from it. Despite his sympathy with Roosevelt's strenuous life, Lodge finally cast his lot with Bigelow's withdrawal. He became what Martin Green has called a Boston aesthete, one who "renounced responsibility for social and political reality—resigned it to the philistines"—and embraced "high culture" as an alternative.[20]

The Boston aesthete was the result of the gradual disintegration during the nineteenth century of the tenuous alliance of business and letters that had underpinned Boston's cultural greatness. By the 1830s, as Lewis P. Simpson has remarked, "an economy of money and a humanistic economy of letters were separate and distinct powers in the Boston community."[21] For most of the nineteenth century, these "economies" were bound together by a "kind of balance of power . . . between the community's dynamic commercial ambitions and its literary aspirations" (59). Only when the Proper Bostonians (the economy of money) and the Brahmins (the economy of letters) split into competing, specialized factions did the decline of Boston's cultural preeminence ensue. By the time of Lodge's career, an aspirant Brahmin could no longer expect the support, either psychological or financial, of Proper Boston. Like W. D. Howells (in Simpson's view), Lodge was "on the one hand . . . compulsively drawn toward idealizing the vocation of the American man of letters, feeling a sacerdotal obligation to represent the literary life as a transcendent, redeeming spiritual order; on the other hand, haunted from the beginning of his career by intimations of doubt about this kind of idealism, he was increasingly disturbed by the feeling that a transcendent frame of reference for American literary life was a meaningless illusion" (91–92). Repulsed by the materialism of Proper Boston, Lodge clung to the Brahmin ideals. But, alienated from Proper Boston, Lodge became a Boston aesthete, a decadent Brahmin who placed a premium on intellectuality and aestheticism for their own sakes, not for the sake of culture at large.

Lodge once attended a White House dinner at which someone

suggested that only about six "really intelligent" men existed in the world. Included on the list was President Roosevelt, but Lodge later revised the list by deleting Roosevelt and adding his father and Henry Adams. Lodge himself aspired to membership in the circle of the "really intelligent," and to this purpose his life became literally an education. Education began, as for most Bostonians of his background, at Harvard College.

IV   At Harvard in the "Golden Age"

Henry Adams described the Harvard he had known in the 1850s as "a mild and liberal school, which sent young men into the world with all they needed to make respectable citizens, and something of what they wanted to make useful ones." The successful Harvard education, as Adams saw it, "resulted in an autobiographical blank, a mind on which only a water-mark had been stamped. . . . It taught little, and that little ill, but it left the mind open, free from bias, ignorant of facts, but docile."[22] During his years at Harvard in the 1870s, however, Henry Cabot Lodge witnessed an educational revolution that eventually transformed the provincial college of the 1850s into a university of national complexion and international outlook. The agent of this revolution was President Charles W. Eliot, who, in the first twenty years of his long tenure, introduced the "elective system." Eliot's idea inverted the traditional philosophy and method at Harvard by shifting the major responsibility for education from the university to the individual student.

To implement the elective system, Eliot assembled an eminent faculty that included in the 1890s such scholars as George Herbert Palmer, Josiah Royce, William James, George Santayana, Charles Eliot Norton, Adams Sherman Hill, Francis J. Child, Ferdinand Bôcher, and Barrett Wendell. The new faculty forced methodological changes during the 1880s; the timeworn daily recitation yielded to the lecture and the seminar. It also undermined the rigid distinction between student and teacher; by the 1890s, many professors routinely opened their homes to their students; and a few, like Caesar de Sumichrast and the legendary Charles T. Copeland, encouraged student-faculty fraternization. While the elective system hastened a breakdown in traditional class unity by dispersing academic interests, the changing pattern of enrollment threatened the social homogeneity of Harvard. The old nucleus of New England students was invaded by regional, ethnic, and religious outsiders who often gained acceptance into the social circles previously dominated by Bostonians.

In retrospect, some alumni painted the 1890s as Harvard's "Golden Age." Norman Hapgood reflected, "If there could be a place intellectually more attractive than Harvard University toward the end of the Nineteenth Century, my imagination does not give it form."[23] Daniel Gregory Mason (Class of '93) recalled, "We were not regimented, standardized, herded, and labelled. We were not intimidated into imitativeness, browbeaten into conformity, or nagged into efficiency. Our healthy nutrition was as little in danger from forced feeding as from starvation; for while we had set before us the feast of the whole of human civilization, what we should take was determined only by our own tastes, appetites, and powers of digestion."[24]

The student of the 1890s may have enjoyed the intellectual feast described by Mason, but he also risked the consequences of indulgence—the collapse of old certainties. Harvard reflected the ferment of the times that could be seen in a series of menacing antinomies: "idealism or materialism, religion or science, human or machine, individual or mob, conservatism or progress, poetry or business, ancient Greece or modern America."[25] At Harvard, sensitive men like George Cabot Lodge frequently turned to poetry as the last repository of humanistic values in an increasingly materialistic society.

George Cabot Lodge passed the Harvard entrance examinations in the summer of 1891 and entered the class of 1895. Besides the required courses in English and chemistry, Lodge elected in his freshman year Latin literature, European history, and two French literature courses. Lodge immediately joined the rowdy Polo Club, and he neglected his studies trying to make the freshman crew. His poor first-semester grades and his parents' subsequent chastisement caused Lodge to complain of being burdened by his father's reputation: "I sometimes wish I did not have such a bright father because I am expected to do so much better than I am able. When [LeBaron Russell] Briggs the English professor who is also the Dean of the college gave me my English mark which was a D he said 'Mr Lodge *you* ought to do much better than that'[;] he evidently has read pa's works and knows about him. Channing the History man also expects a great deal of me because I am the son of my father."[26] Lodge continued to labor in his father's shadow, and his work during his first two years was mediocre enough to place him on probation.

Fortunately, one course excited him. Philosophy 1, taught by Palmer, Royce, and Santayana, introduced Lodge to idealistic philosophy; and he immediately fell under the spell of Thomas Carlyle. "I have read attentively almost everything he ever wrote except Cromwell & I am taking notes on all the more philosophical ones like Sartor Resartus and I am also reading & studying conjointly the French philosophers Descartes[,] Malebranche, & Spinoza & the German Schopenhauer & Fichte & also Plato so that I shall get an Idea of his relations to the celebrated philosophies."[27]

Lodge entered his junior year with a schedule more suited to his interests: two courses in French literature, two in history, and one in fine arts, as well as Santayana's seminar in aesthetics. In Professor Sumichrast's course, Lodge developed a lasting distaste for Realism, and for the work of Paul Bourget in particular. "I feel as if I had been living in the mire. Never have I read books whose atmosphere was so unhealthy and fetid."[28] Shaken and challenged by his readings, Lodge suffered periodic depressions. Echoing Charles Eliot Norton's rejection of the age, Lodge wrote to his mother, "I feel like de Musset 'je suis venu trop tard dans un monde trop vieux': All of human society seems to me to be in a tense, nervous condition which must break. . . . We are now passing through the worst stage. When the crash comes there will at least be action and not the rapid impotency, the unbroken mediocrity of the present day. Carlyle's Shrieks of distress have become very prophetic sounds."[29] Despite his mood or because of it, Lodge plunged into his studies with unprecedented enthusiasm. "I have been reading an immense quantity from variegated authors, Balzac specially also Flaubert, Alfred de Vigny, Leconte de Lisle, Musset, Hugo, Renan (whom I am going to write a long french theme about) Schopenhauer, the Upanishads etc. . . ."[30]

In his senior year, Lodge concentrated almost exclusively on French literature, electing three courses with Professor Bôcher. He also studied Schopenhauer under Royce and eighteenth-century English literature with Lewis Gates (Frank Norris's mentor). Released from probation in May, 1894, Lodge began to master his studies and to write poetry. Throughout the winter and spring of 1895, he mailed his poems home as soon as they were written. His father, relieved perhaps to find his son's education taking a direction, patiently criticized and in some cases rewrote them. At his father's suggestion, Lodge attempted imitations of French Symbolist poetry, but he gradually turned to the Petrarchan sonnet for a literary model. Even in his earliest work, Lodge showed an impatience with revision that derived in part from his belief in the Romantic doctrine of inspiration. "I find I cannot polish my verses to any great extent. I write when I feel in the mood & then they are done—badly or well, as the case may be. If badly they must either be all written over or else burnt and a new one written—generally the most appropriate fate for most of them."[31]

Senator Lodge proudly showed his son's fledgling efforts to Theodore Roosevelt. With his usual impetuosity, Roosevelt insisted on immediate publication and submitted a sonnet, with Lodge's consent, to Richard Watson Gilder of the *Century*. Gilder's rejection did not discourage Roosevelt from sponsoring Lodge's career elsewhere over the next few years. In 1896, for example, Roosevelt thrust "The Song of the Wave" upon Edward Burlingame, editor of *Scribner's*. "Burlingame jumped at the chance of seeing 'The Wave,' and told me that he was sincerely obliged to me for giving him the opportunity," Roosevelt confided to Henry Cabot Lodge. "He meant this, for he repeated it three or four times, saying that he considered himself under a personal obligation, because he felt that 'young Lodge' was doing noteworthy work, and he told me to write and have it sent on at once, being evidently afraid that some other Magazine would get the first choice. . . . Let me know what Burlingame says about 'The Wave.' What he says, I may mention, will affect merely my opinion of him, not of the poem."[32] Roosevelt's success in pressuring magazine editors undoubtedly advanced Lodge's career, but it encouraged him to publish before he was sure of his craft. *The Song of the Wave and Other Poems*, even though delayed in publication until 1898, was marred by immaturity and haste.

While his father and his patron exercised their influence to launch him as a magazine poet, Lodge aimed for the more personal and immediate success of publication in the *Harvard Monthly*. Founded by George Santayana and his friends in 1885, the *Monthly* had become by 1895 the testing ground for aspiring Harvard poets. Its editorial board during Lodge's years included William Vaughn Moody, Norman Hapgood, Hugh McCulloch, Philip Savage, Charles Macomb Flandrau, and Joseph Trumbull Stickney, who was to become Lodge's closest friend. More than Henry Cabot Lodge or Roosevelt, Stickney inspired Lodge's literary hopes.

Trumbull Stickney had grown up in Europe and had come to Harvard with intellectual maturity and sophistication beyond his years. While Lodge flirted with probation, Stickney maintained a high average in Harvard's demanding classics curriculum. More important, at the time he met Lodge in May, 1894, Stickney had joined the undergraduate literati. In 1892, he became the first freshman ever elected to the board of the *Harvard Monthly*, and during the next years almost every issue included one or more of his poems. Lodge found in Stickney an intellectual soulmate who shared his aspirations as well as his disillusionments, and each man complemented perfectly the other's personality. Through Stickney, Lodge met the other senior members of the *Monthly* board. Thanks in part to these connections, Lodge succeeded in publishing one of his sonnets in the *Monthly*. The poem, which Lodge later revised and entitled "Nirvana," appeared without title and anonymously in the May, 1895, issue.

In his last semester, Lodge began to envision himself as a poet, but he as yet lacked confidence in his ability. "I am dévoré by ambition. I do so want and long to do something that will last—some man's work in the world that I am constantly depressed by an awful dread that perhaps I shan't be able to. I am never satisfied with what I do—never contented with my expression of what I wish to express, and yet I hope and sometimes feel that it is possible I may do something permanent in value."[33] At commencement, the class poem by Charles Macomb Flandrau articulated the anxiety Lodge struggled to express in this letter: the fear that poetry would prove to be an impotent weapon with which to confront the perplexing reality of life outside college. Flandrau chided the

> Nobly deluded youth that sought to wring
>   From bloodless books the knowledge that is power
>   Until his yellow cresset in the tower
> Flared pale before the sun-gate's opening;
>
> And you, small scriveners, that dare to ply
>   Your little pens, and are so fond to think
>   'Tis mirrored in a drop of feeble ink
> How fellow-creatures love and live and die;
>
> And you who battle more with men and less
>   With arid words . . .[34]

The tension implicit in Flandrau's poem between words and action would underlie Lodge's severe emotional crises in Paris the next year. If, as the pessimism sweeping Harvard in the 1890s had it,

society regards poetry as "arid words," then it followed that art and
society were essentially incompatible, and that society was an
enemy to the artist. Schopenhauer had plainly said, "If a man wants
to go down to posterity [or in Lodge's words, to "do something
permanent in value"], he must withdraw from the influence of his
own age. This will, of course, generally mean that he must also
renounce any influence upon it, and be ready to buy centuries of
fame by foregoing the applause of his contemporaries."[35]
    A striking version of this *fin de siècle* commonplace appeared in
the *Harvard Monthly* in 1886 in the form of an imaginary conversation between Arthur Phaulophilanthropos and Margites Chitterly:

A.P.   Well, Margites, how are you?
M.C.   Degenerating.
A.P.   That is sad. What's the matter?
M.C.   You know. The country's the matter. One can't grow here, unless
        one waits to grow up with the country.
A.P.   I'm afraid that would be slow work. . . . And what is your conclu-
        sion?
M.C.   That artistic development is all but impossible in this country. Ev-
        erything here is for the million, and those who, like artists, are not
        of the million, have to go to the wall. You may make your fortune
        here, you may win fame in this, that or the other way, but you can
        never find art.[36]

Although Lodge had not reached this conclusion for himself at Harvard, he would emerge from his year in Paris firm in the belief that,
as a poet, he must both fight the million and be its martyr.

CHAPTER 2

The Song of the Wave
and Other Poems

IN 1895, when Lodge joined Stickney at the Sorbonne, Paris was
teeming with artists and writers who jammed the cafés along "le
Boul' Mich' " in search of gay times and perhaps a glimpse of Paul
Verlaine or Stéphane Mallarmé. To the young writer, Paris's legendary Bohemian subculture promised freedom from conventionality
and a test of artistic mettle; and Lodge wanted above all to prove his
worth as a poet.

As Henry Adams suggested of his own European experience,
education perhaps was best accomplished not in the classroom but
in the cafés, billiard halls, and theaters; education was "accidental,
unintended, unforeseen."[1] Lodge expected to study Romance lan
guages, but the Sorbonne catalyzed a learning process more personal and painful. For the first time, Lodge escaped the immediate
influence of his parents and Boston society; but "accidental education" intensified the anxieties of his Harvard days. His perturbations
underlay the tone of disillusionment and restlessness in his first
volume of poems.

I Accidental Education in Paris and Berlin

Lodge hoped that a year's study in Paris would prepare him for a
position at Harvard that would provide income to underwrite a
literary career. Lodge proposed to take eighteen courses (mostly in
French literature and culture), to write a thesis in order to compress
into one year the two-year course for the *degré d'études
supérieures*, and to learn German and Italian while improving his
Latin and Spanish. Impressed at first by the specialized scholarship
of his professors, he labored diligently at his thesis about the French
poet Octavien de St-Gélays. Within a month, however, Lodge be-

31

came disenchanted: "The teuton has invaded Paris as well as Harvard & other places of learning & literature as such is more & more giving place to philology & text criticism. In a short thesis like mine a literary essay would be laughed at. You must be dull & learned & philological unless you have a large book to write in which you can totally exhaust all aspects of your subject."[2]

Frustration with philology masked a deeper anxiety. Disturbed by reading Brooks Adams's *Law of Civilization and Decay* and its pessimistic conclusions about poetry in the modern world, Lodge professed to his mother:

I abhor my incapacity for faith, my utter Scepticism, all that makes of me a man of this end of the 19th century. . . . Personally I can live a very happy life I dare say. I have my poets & cathedrals etc to make me happy & fortunately I want very little money. To earn that very little & to write down my thoughts & publish them—voilà all I ask to do. I don't expect to be heard or listened to much or to get much reputation to myself. I want to say my little say with as strong & loud voice as I can and say it simply, directly, & if possible well & that's all.[3]

Lodge embraced in this and other letters to his parents, the idea that poetry would isolate him from the mainstream of his time and, more significantly, fail to provide him with financial security. Consequently, he believed a literary career depended on his ability to enter academic life. As his enthusiasm for "teutonic" scholarship dissipated, the conflict between his desire to write poetry and his need to earn a living intensified. Moreover, his distress was compounded by a political crisis that challenged his sense not only of self but of nationalism.

During the winter of 1894–95, a simmering boundary dispute between Venezuela and British Guiana exploded when gold was discovered in the disputed territory. The United States Senate, anticipating a collision of British and American interests in South America, passed a resolution that both parties should submit to American arbitration. Venezuela readily agreed, but England ignored this intrusion into its affairs. In the summer of 1895, President Grover Cleveland escalated the resolution into an ultimatum in his "twenty-inch gun" speech. On December 17, the President told a joint session of Congress that the United States should arbitrate the dispute regardless of British interests and then enforce the settlement. Cleveland's speech released a war fever that quickly infected Lodge in Paris. While his father was invoking the Monroe

Doctrine on the floor of Congress to support Cleveland's policy, Lodge, feeling hopelessly removed, could find no one sympathetic to his views. "Yesterday I read Cleveland's message to congress & today I read that Congress has supported him & that the whole nation is behind Congress. My State of mind is almost apoplectic."[4]

In the next few days, Lodge began to recognize that personal insecurities rather than the Venezuela affair had brought him to the brink of nervous collapse. The root of his crisis, as revealed in long letters to his always understanding mother, was guilt about placing his poetic aspirations above practical considerations:

I said to myself that I ought to go home in order to get into the tide of American life if for nothing else that I oughtn't to be dreaming & shrieking inside & poetizing & labouring on literature here in Paris supported by my father & that I ought to go home & live very hard making money. I said to myself that I knew I could not be very quick at money-making but that at any rate in the eyes of men I should lead a selfrespecting life & my hideous, utter failure would only be for myself & you. . . . But somehow all the while my soul refused to believe the plain facts & illogically clung to the belief that I might do some good & creative work in the world after all. . . . [5]

The conflict Lodge felt between words and action, between poetry and money-making, ultimately between the world of art and the world of Boston society, was to pervade both his work and his life. Although he tried desperately to resolve the tensions, he would choose finally to abandon action, money-making, and Boston altogether.

Throughout the winter of 1896, Lodge wrote prolifically, and his lagging spirits were raised by the coming of Parisian spring and by the acceptance of one sonnet each by *Scribner's* and *Harper's*. Late in the spring, Lodge decided to abandon his work for a degree and to return home. But reimmersion in American society only aggravated Lodge's alienation from it. He had complained of the American colony in Paris, "I know of no animal of whatever nationality so utterly odious as the denationalized American."[6] But the Americans he encountered at Newport repulsed him even more: "I hate the philistine-plutocrat atmosphere of this place, and it tends not to diminish my views anent modern civilization and the money power. I sincerely thank God I shall never be a rich man, and never will I, if my strength holds. The world cannot be fought with its own weapons. David fought Goliath with a sling, and the only way to kill the world is to fight it with one's own toy sword or sling, and deny strenuously contact with, or participation in, the power it cherishes."[7] Ironically, Lodge could not at the moment have compromised with the "money power" if he had wished; his degreeless year at Paris fitted him for no profession. When his hopes of a Harvard appointment evaporated, Lodge decided, with his father's consent, to return to Europe to continue his studies. He chose Berlin in order to learn German and to explore the German philosophy that had interested him since Harvard.

To Henry Adams, the Berlin he had known in 1858 was a "poor, keen-witted, provincial town, simple, dirty, uncivilized, and in most respects disgusting."[8] The apparent lack of culture in Berlin amazed Lodge from the start. "The appalling extinction of all thought & art here gives an opportunity to criticism. It's unbelievable. Sudermann & Hauptman (very mediocre) is literally all the literature of any kind there is. Philosophy is dead[,] despised, art is not, & music dies with Brahms. The whole German nation is devoted with that peculiar German thoroughness to moneymaking & commercial science."[9] Brooks Adams had encouraged Lodge to write prose as a way to build a literary reputation while achieving financial independence. Lodge heeded the advice and, with his father's help, obtained the status of unofficial Berlin correspondent for the New York *Sun*. On his first assignment he eagerly reviewed Hermann Sudermann's *Morituri*, which Lodge felt epitomized the artistic bankruptcy of Realism.

Lodge began with a wry summary of Sudermann's popular novel *Frau Sorge*: "The background . . . is a wide flat sandy plain whose chief characteristic is that it is allways gray. The Sun rarely shines in Realism. When this plain is not swathed in an unhealthy mist one realizes that it is inhabited. The exigencies of realism require that the inhabitants should be either peasants or prostitutes. Let us be thankful that in this case they are peasants, peasants, however, whose brutal stupidity we trust is not matched in nature." Lodge used Sudermann to denounce other realistic writers (Bourget, Gabriele D'Annunzio, and Howells) and their defender Brander Matthews: "And indeed what is this realism, this literature of the intelligent & virtuous? How does it differ from the Imaginative, primitive literature which according to Mr. Matthews is responsible for every crime from the Spanish Inquisition to the Civil War? Is not the difference perhaps this: that Sudermann & D'Annunzio are realists

not because they are truer to life than Scott but because they have
less imagination. . . . If one can't be Goethe one must be Sudermann." Drawing upon the theories of decadence of Max Nordau and
Brooks Adams, Lodge blamed the decline of German culture on the
rise of commercialism: "Everything from God Almighty to the
drama has a commercial value & none other. Thus interest in art[,]
literature or science for their own sakes has departed."[10]
  Lodge turned in February to a review of Jules Huret's *Enquête
sur la Question Sociale en Europe.* Relying again on Adams's *Law of
Civilization and Decay,* Lodge argued that the ultimate consequence of socialism is not a proletarian state but anarchy: "As
Malatesta the anarchist says: there are but two solutions to the
present state of affairs—cessation of progress & anarchy. Therefore
the Socialists & all other discontented persons are in fact Anarchists.
Whoever does not wish to preserve the Social conditions of today
untouched & stationary is aiming at their destruction. He may call
himself Collectivist, Socialist or radical but in fact he is an anarchist."[11]
  Though Lodge had no sympathy with its political forms, he allied
himself with anarchism which was theoretically and broadly
defined as resistance to "progress" and to the social assumptions of
commercialism. Charles Dana, editor of the *Sun,* could hardly spon-
sor such subversive ideas; and when Lodge's article appeared in
print, it had been deftly edited. Outraged, Lodge accused Dana of
overstepping his editorial authority. "I'm sorry it was printed for it
has been so much cut that it is now an ardent defence of modern
civilization & a condemnation of any one who is discontented which
I don't think it was in the original form & which it certainly wasn't
intended to be."[12] He not only refused payment for the review but
declined to write further for the *Sun.*
  The winter in Berlin became a productive period for poetry. Re-
veling in solitude, Lodge began to feel a competence in his work
that was reflected in a new self-confidence in his letters. During two
months Lodge wrote dozens of poems, half of which he would include in his first volume.

  II   The Song of the Wave *and "The Genteel Tradition"*

  The Song of the Wave and Other Poems, which appeared in December, 1898, grew from Lodge's experiences at Harvard, Paris,
and Berlin. Like many first volumes, it was something of a miscel-

lany. From his work since 1894, Lodge collected about seventy-five short poems, of which three-fifths were sonnets. Also like many first volumes, *The Song of the Wave* was derivative; reviewers detected echoes and borrowings from Giacomo Leopardi (to whom the book was dedicated), Schopenhauer, Leconte de Lisle, Robert Browning, William Ernest Henley, A. C. Swinburne, Emerson, Sidney Lanier, and Walt Whitman. But, if Lodge owed much to literary tradition, he also demonstrated his willingness to experiment with a variety of styles and forms, and thus to adapt tradition to his own uses.

Senator Lodge agreed to underwrite the publication of the book when Bay returned from Europe in 1897. Above all, the father wanted his son's work to carry the imprint of a prestigious house, and he promised Scribner's that his son's poems contained "nothing in them which you could possibly object to being associated with your name as publisher."[13] Ironically, Lodge would have expected some of his poems, especially the jeremiads to modern society, to offend a respectable publisher. Like some of the reviewers of *The Song of the Wave,* Scribner's may have regarded Lodge's pessimism as a youthful phase.

Senator Lodge reacted to the poems with guarded optimism. "I think there is a note of decided promise in some of them which indicates a prospect of good work in his maturity," he told Roosevelt. Roosevelt, however, voiced unqualified approval: "As for Bay's poems, as you know, I think he has the 'touch of the purple' in him."[14] The most hostile reviewer of *The Song of the Wave* detected instead a touch of the purple passage: "We have glimpses of Kipling . . . and of Browning and of Leopardi—and, above all, of youth and its ardor and its crudeness. . . . The enormous gilded wave which overspreads the cover of this book . . . give[s] a promise of something turgid and rhetorical, whose pledge the book itself . . . does something to fulfill."[15]

In the *Dial,* William Morton Payne complained that Lodge lacked "the saving sense of humor," but he also agreed with Senator Lodge: "Mr. Lodge's work seems to us to be full of promise; its utterance is large, and its rhythmic power is undeniable."[16] The anonymous reviewer in the *Harvard Graduates Magazine* refused to ridicule what he saw as the vulnerable immaturity of the volume: "While Mr. Lodge seems to us . . . to indulge too often in extravagances of expression, and to lack at times definiteness of phrase and the clear

thought behind, he has intellectual vigor and the courage of his
convictions, which make a hopeful foundation for future work."[17]
    Howard Mumford Jones has called *The Song of the Wave* an
example of "The Genteel Tradition" in American poetry, and it
illuminates Lodge's first volume to examine it against the assumptions of a particular genteel tradition.[18] As Edwin H. Cady has
pointed out, "Since Dickens 'genteel' has connoted the fussy, pre-
tentious, shallow, and ignorant imitation of gentility which is vulgarity seven times compounded."[19] Applied to intellectual contexts by
George Santayana in his term "The Genteel Tradition," "genteel"
retained all its pejorative connotations. After Santayana used the
phrase to characterize American philosophy in 1911, many social
and literary critics, including Santayana himself, stretched "The
Genteel Tradition" indiscriminately.
    The term became a convenient weapon with which to bludgeon
every unfashionable aspect of American culture. As a result, "The
Genteel Tradition" has come to defy precise definition. Cady has
suggested the permanent adoption of Vernon L. Parrington's general definition: a genteel tradition is "a timid and uncreative culture
that lays its inhibitions on every generation that is content to live
upon the past."[20] Lodge was trapped in a poetic genteel tradition by
his failure to escape the inhibiting conventions of English Romantic
poetry. For Lodge and his contemporaries, the old orthodoxies of
poetry had decayed with other nineteenth-century certainties. By
1900, as Frederick Eckman has argued, the Romantic tradition of
poetic language "was no longer a stimulating, fruitful tradition."[21]
    Eckman has identified four somewhat contradictory modes of
Romantic poetic theory that informed the practice of nineteenth-
century English and American poets. The poet in the "emotional
mode" believed that poetry had "its source in inspiration and its
highest purpose in the expression of moral idealism. The proper
tone of poetry was thought to be emotional; hence a language of
strong affective connotations came to be sanctioned. . . . This already indefinite language of connotation gradually became even
more vague (as well as more conventional) by reason of indifference
to careful word choice and sentence structure" (4–5).
    Counter to this "emotional mode," Eckman distinguishes three
modes that stressed the poet's careful attention to language. The
poet in the "concretive mode" attempted to replace "intellectual
abstractions with imagery" so as to treat "ideas through the medium

of objects"(47). The "euphonic mode" emphasized the "musical values of language sounds" and advocated at its extreme that "poetry should try to emulate the absolute aural beauty of music and to dissociate itself from meaning" (47, 23). Finally, the "idiomatic mode" championed "a deliberate return to plain, colloquial speech" and to the use of poetic language "appropriate to the emotions or ideas expressed" (4–5, 22).

Throughout most of the nineteenth century, these four modes coexisted in various proportions in the work of major English and American poets. Poetics late in the century placed increasing emphasis on the emotional mode, and poetry in which this mode predominated may be called genteel. A revolt against genteel American poetry, led at first by Amy Lowell and Ezra Pound, began to gather strength in the early decades of the twentieth century. *Poetry: A Magazine of Verse* was founded in 1912 as an organ of the new poetry, variously called Imagism, *Imagisme*, and Vorticism. Whatever its rightful name, the three tenets of the movement were not in question:

1. Direct treatment of the "thing," whether subjective or objective.
2. To use absolutely no word that did not contribute to the presentation.
3. As regarding rhythm: to compose in sequence of the musical phrase, not in sequence of a metronome.[22]

In Eckman's terms, the Imagist Movement represented a reassertion of the concretive, idiomatic, and euphonic modes in poetry, and a rejection of the emotional mode. Indeed, T. S. Eliot later added a fourth tenet of Imagism and of most modern poetry when he insisted: "Poetry is not a turning loose of emotion, but an escape from emotion; it is not the expression of personality, but an escape from personality. . . . The emotion of art is impersonal."[23]

Eckman categorizes Lodge, Stickney, and Moody as transitional poets, torn between the lure of a genteel Romantic tradition and their awareness of the need for new poetic forms and language. Unlike E. A. Robinson, W. B. Yeats, or Pound, these three poets never completely outgrew their dependence on the poetic genteel tradition, and their work exhibited a commixture of Imagistic and genteel elements. "All of them worked toward freshness and originality of expression; but for each there was an irresistable urge to return . . . to the easily available comforts of Romantic diction.

Their indecision about language was so acute, in fact, that it caused unevenness not merely between poems but frequently between parts of a poem" (140). This unevenness is everywhere in *The Song of the Wave,* and a typical example is the sonnet "Aux Modernes":

> Only an empty platitude for God,
> Only for poetry a jangling nerve,
> Only for life the baser lusts to serve,
> Only a fashion where the function stood.
> Only a shadow stealing span on span
>   Over the unmeasured whiteness of the soul;
>   Darkness around the God-established goal
>   That blazed before the innocence of man.
> And when the flame of adolescence breaks
>   On some wild heart the world has overthrown,
>   He stares as one who waits alone and wakes,
> Cheated of love and faith, his vision drawn
> Haggard and hopeless from his death-bed down
> The hard, gray, tacit distances of dawn.

> (I, 95)

Inflated diction clashes in this poem with the economic language of Imagism. The concreteness of "for poetry a jangling nerve" jars against the mistiness of "the unmeasured whiteness of the soul."

In his apprentice volume, Lodge shared many of the assumptions of the emotional mode that underlay genteel American poetry. He believed in the doctrine of inspiration. "I never do force myself to write," he told his father in 1896. "In fact, I couldn't. I don't believe verse does force itself. You can't write till you have to which to my mind is one of the blessed things about it."[24] Throughout his career Lodge wanted his poetry to express the loftiest idealism, and he regarded the role of poet as sacred: "If I have it in me to be a real poet I should be endlessly happy but it's reaching to the highest thing I can Imagine & It seems almost a presumption to expect or even hope it."[25] Lodge also felt that the basis of poetry must be powerful emotion. When an artist friend tried to convince Lodge "that art ought to be without feeling & entirely scientific & that Manet was as great a painter as Titian & in some ways greater," Lodge retorted that, "if one was soulless, emotionless & nothing in

God's world but a combination of little bugs it would seem more sensible to leave art alone."[26]

Because Lodge used poetry as a vehicle for cosmic ideas, he often fell into the trap of the emotional mode—"the feeling that if an idea has sufficient emotional impetus, it will provide its own words."[27] He admired that quality he found in Kant and Schopenhauer and described as "a white purity consisting in its utter lack of connection to the particular, in its entire devotion to the pure, synthetical ideas which never touch the feeling, individual world, which makes metaphysics the nearest approach to will-lessness, to pure intellectual contemplation, that I know."[28] If, as Lodge thought, poetry should be a vehicle for metaphysics, then the poet must necessarily strive for a "white purity" of language. The powerful emotion underlying a given poem must depend for expression not on concrete images but on the language of metaphysical abstraction.

The consequences of this poetics are apparent in the sonnet "Nirvana II," written in December, 1897. Characteristically, Lodge undertook to describe the abstract through the abstract:

> Woof of the scenic sense, large monotone
>   Where life's diverse inceptions, death and birth,
>   Where all the gaudy overflow of earth,
>   Merge—they the manifold and thou the One.
> Increate, complete—when the stars are gone
>   In cinders down the void, when yesterday
>   No longer spurs desire starvation-gray,
>   When God grows mortal in men's hearts of stone,—
> As each pulsation of the Heart Divine
>   Peoples the chaos, or with falling breath
>   Beggars creation, still the soul is thine!
> And still untortured by the world's increase,
>   Thy wide, harmonic silences of death;
>   And last—thy white uncovered breast of peace.
>
> (I, 81)

The poem is constructed entirely of mixed metaphors and words utterly lacking concreteness: "monotone," "inceptions," "gaudy," "increate," "Heart Divine," "harmonic silences," "white uncovered breast of peace." Lodge complained to Bigelow of his frustration in writing "Nirvana II" that "I wrote it without correction in half an hour before dinner, and I feel of it, as I have felt of so many things,

that no one will understand it except you; also I know it's my fault
and not theirs that no one will understand it—my implements are
still so rude—my ideas seem luminous and limpid while they are
wordless . . . but in words they become crude, misty, and imperfect." Lodge attached a prose paraphrase of the sonnet, but even in
prose he was not fully articulate. "This is of course a mere shadow-
ing forth of the ideas I had in writing the poem. You will see their
possible amplifications," he assured Bigelow.[29] But Lodge could not
expect every reader to be as sympathetic as Bigelow or Roosevelt,
who professed that he greatly admired the sonnet "After" although
he was "not absolutely clear what it is about!"[30]

Lodge wanted desperately to communicate the powerful emotions that struggled mutely behind his poems. He wrote to his
mother in 1897, "All my life is comprised in my verse for it has to
take the place of human intercourse & all other forms of expression."[31] Yet Lodge was painfully aware that, despite his efforts,
many of his poems suggested rather than expressed his meaning. He
published "Nirvana II" without revision, perhaps in deference to
the sanctity of its inspiration, but also perhaps in acknowledgment of
his inability to clarify it.

III *A Soul-history*

It is easy to find weaknesses in *The Song of the Wave*. Maurice
Brown has mercilessly dissected one of the sonnets to show Lodge
tripping over his tangled syntax, and Thomas Riggs has insisted that
"long passages of it can stand little critical examination."[32] But
Lodge did achieve groping power and technical ingenuity in several
poems that merit more sympathetic attention. What distinguished
the best poems in *The Song of the Wave* from genteel American
poetry was their insistent tone of disillusionment. If in his forms and
language he resembled romantic models, in his denunciation of the
spiritual sterility of modern culture Lodge anticipated T. S. Eliot's
The Waste Land. As Larzer Ziff has said of Lodge, Stickney, and
Moody, "They felt the contradiction between science as light-
bringer and science as destroyer of humane values, and their poetry
was filled with imagery inspired by the notion of their living at the
twilight of the century. The world of their poetry in the nineties is a
darkening and chilly sphere, and their search for values is a search
for a light-bringer."[33]

The wasteland theme pervades *The Song of the Wave;* throughout
there is

> A sense of falling leaves through gray linked rain,
> Of perished youth with grave prophetic eyes
> And strange scant visions of a hopeless past.
>
> (I, 15)

In one of Lodge's best sonnets, the choking "Fog at Sea" prefigures
the fog that swirls through Eliot's "The Love Song of J. Alfred
Prufrock":

> Gray grisly tides that choke the master sun
>   Who domes the caves of sullen fog with pearl,
>   While round and still the sick white eddies swirl
>   Between the smothered vistas one by one;
> Like ghosts the frail hysteric breezes run
>   Aslant the ashen world, and strive to furl
>   The slow drenched air in one enormous whirl
>   And free the ocean's breast it weighs upon.
> The world is dying for a draught of air,
>   Great autumn air that like a hoarded stream
>   Floods the gigantic openness of dawn;
> And, like the whispering of hopeless prayer,
>   The white world's voices, as if drowsed with dream,
>   Sigh through the muffled stillness and are gone.
>
> (I, 79)

But if Lodge's intention is to portray the suffocation of "the white
world's voices," he also wants to find hope:

> If I must live,
> And feel the ashes of oblivion
> ˏAbout my soul,
> Let life be fearful, let me feel the whole,
> Despair, and face the sunrise—if I grieve
> Let it but be the tarrying of the sun.
>
> (I, 51)

Lodge intended *The Song of the Wave* to chart his own search for
values: his spiritual odyssey from innocent hope through despairing
consciousness of the twilight of his age to a chastened belief in the

transcending self. In 1897 Lodge wrote to his mother, "All my life since last April I have been going over, as I have some of my poems, forcing the events into sequence and building a sort of soul-history, fibrous and coherent."[34] Although *The Song of the Wave* does not have a clearly defined development from poem to poem, it does suggest in its overall impetus a "soul-history" of the passage from innocence to experience.

Lodge's philosophical premise in the volume was a Schopenhauerian inversion of Emerson: "As all suffering is willful (in the essential meaning) and emotional, pure intellectual contemplation must be that privation of suffering in which happiness consists—for I become more than ever convinced that in this world of evil and separation happiness is only the privation of pain as good is the privation of evil. 'Tis only the transcendent emotion that you get in poetry or in great passions such as pity and love, that can be called positive happiness."[35] Lodge's quest in *The Song of the Wave* was happiness through a poetry of vitality and assertion in a decaying, autumnal world that counseled silence and submission.

In the volume, Lodge juxtaposed his jeremiads to society to his celebrations of transcendence. In the opening poem, the poet's soul begs him to sing even "if it be an echo of thy dread, / A dirge of hope, of young illusions dead— / Perchance God hears!" (I, 3). As Lodge makes clear, however, God, or at least the God of traditional religion, is dead; and modern man must regain the primitive insight of the Norsemen:

> These are the men!
> In their youth without memory
> They were glad, for they might not see
> The lies that the world has wrought
> On this parchment of God. The tree
> Yielded them ships and the sky
> Flamed as the waters fought;
> But they knew that death was a lie,
> That the life of man was as nought,
> And they dwelt in the truth of the sea:
> These are the men!
>   (I, 13–14)

In nature, from the breath of "The East Wind," man may still learn the old lesson of self-divinity.

To me
  The whisper came, the voice and then the call
  Of wanton power, and then, o'erwhelming all,
  The passion of mine own infinity.

                                         (I, 11)

Nature offers the poet harmony. As the Ocean tells him,

  "Come," said the Ocean, "if thy soul is fit
  To bear my mastery, thy words shall flow
  Simple and adequate as human tears,
  And all thy discord fall in great accords."

                                          (I, 4)

The cost of harmony, however, is isolation and silence. The song
of the Ocean is ultimately a wordless hymn of solipsism:

  Take my beauty—God's image is mirrored,
    Take my pity for Fate's sure control,
  Take my song, it is Life's evanescence,
    Take my silence, the strength of the Soul!

                                          (I, 6)

The poet chooses instead the song of the wave and the song of the
sword; that is, he elects to prophesy his transcendental vision to a
decadent society even if, as he expects, society will ignore him. Like
the wave, the poet's words shatter into "infinite atoms" upon the
shore of unheeding society; and the poet's reward is not a "fillet of
morning stars" but death:

  This is the song of the wave, that died in the fulness of life.
  The prodigal this, that lavished its largess of strength
      In the lust of attainment.
  Aiming at things for Heaven too high,
  Sure in the pride of life, in the richness of strength.
  So tried it the impossible height, till the end was found:
  Where ends the soul that yearns for the fillet of morning stars,
  The soul in the toils of the journeying worlds,
  Whose eye is filled with the Image of God,
      And the end is Death!

                                          (I, 9)

Lodge came to doubt the efficacy of poetry as a means of communicating with society and to regard it more as a means of finding the transcendent self. The volume ended with another exhortation for the poet's soul, which promises:

> Thy royal heart shall cross the wide-eyed dawn
> Alone, and find the unspoken thing I am
> Waiting for none but thee behind the sham
> Of rhymèd words where the poem's self is born.
>
> (I, 114)

These lines raise the question of audience in Lodge's work. If poetry is a "sham of rhymèd words," if the goal of poetry is the unspeakable comprehension of the soul's infinity, then to whom does the poem communicate except to the poet himself? Lodge's worst poetry became an inner dialogue, inaccessible to the reader. Because they are more concrete and accessible, the poems in which Lodge defined the worldly evils he rejected are better than those in which he described the transcendental quest. The best poems in *The Song of the Wave*—the title poem, "The East Wind," "Fall," "Fog at Sea"—are invariably lyrics of nature. Thus, Lodge's strength as a poet was directly contrary to his own poetics: so far as his poems succeeded as metaphysical contemplations, they failed as poems.

IV A Working Arrangement Between Beacon Street and the Universe

If *The Song of the Wave* was, as Adams suggested, Lodge's "first public act of divorce," its posture of revolt did not solve "the extremely practical problem of effecting some sort of working arrangement between Beacon Street and the universe."[36] The volume sold poorly, and Lodge scarcely recovered its production costs. Unable to subsist as a poet, Lodge went to Washington in 1897 as private secretary to his father, a job he held for the rest of his life. The need to earn a living forced upon him a double existence: Senate work during the day; writing poetry at night, often into the morning hours. Although he did not neglect his secretarial duties, he dispatched them with little enthusiasm; and the existence of manuscript poems on Senate stationery suggest that his night's work intruded upon his daytime activities.

Life in Washington did allow frequent contact with his father's close friends—especially Adams, Roosevelt, and John Hay—and the formation of new friendships with Edith Wharton and Charles Warren Stoddard. Lodge's relationship with Stoddard epitomized the limitations of the Washington set. Like Roosevelt, Stoddard became a mentor who overlooked the deficiencies in Lodge's poetry; but Lodge needed encouragement tempered with criticism. Instead, the blind encouragement of his circle retarded his development. Years later, Edith Wharton acutely assessed the effect of the Washington set on Lodge. "He grew up in a hot-house of intensive culture," she wrote, "and was one of the most complete examples I have ever known of the young genius before whom an adoring family unites in smoothing the way. This kept him out of the struggle of life, and consequently out of its experiences, and to the end his intellectual precocity was combined with a boyishness of spirit at once delightful and pathetic."[37]

Lodge escaped Washington briefly to serve, during the Spanish-American War, as a gunnery officer aboard his uncle's ship, the *Dixie*. Captain Charles Henry Davis reported proudly to Henry Cabot Lodge that young Lodge showed "unbounded zeal and unflagging industry, and a great aptitude for the profession."[38] In retrospect, some of the Lodges felt that Lodge's happiest days were those aboard the *Dixie*, and he obviously enjoyed the challenge and power of command. "It's a great business to be here & see the wheels go round & be a wheel oneself even if not a very big one," he wrote to his parents.[39] In combat, Lodge felt a sense of security and accomplishment he would never gain from his poetry; but, despite his promotion to ensign at the end of the war, he rejected a military career. "I came for the war & as this isn't & never will be my life when the war is over I want to get home as soon as possible. . . . I haven't seen as much fighting as some but I've had my share of the fun I think & anyway one does one's best & takes the chances of war. I really think I've made myself useful & at least have not encumbered or hurt the Service by coming & that's as much as an amateur can hope for."[40] If Lodge thought himself an amateur at war, he desperately wanted to establish his professionalism as a writer.

The achievement of this goal was made more urgent by his engagement, during 1899, to Elizabeth Frelinghuysen Davis, a beautiful Washington debutante from a family distinguished by generations of prominent public officials. The Davises were not enchanted by the prospect of a poet son-in-law; and, in the years 1899–1900,

Lodge, under pressure from the Davises, tried to write plays and novels that might bring commercial success. When E. C. Stedman, who included "The Song of the Wave" in his *American Anthology*, asked Lodge for biographical information, he responded hopefully, "I have neither business or profession except literature."[41] However, except for small payments from the magazines, Lodge had yet to earn anything from his literary efforts.

During a trip to Europe in 1899, Lodge dutifully began a novel; but he complained after finishing it, "Apart from its possible tho' problematical value as a gagne-pain the book hardly interests me."[42] Writing novels forced Lodge to neglect his poetry and threatened to compromise his convictions of society's corruption. Lodge felt that a novel that reflected his true feelings could never be published and certainly would not sell if it were. Conversely, a novel palatable to the audience Lodge imagined for fiction would be a lie. "I'm almost crazed with the desire to be independent," he wrote his mother; "and yet I won't do anything that I don't approve and I won't give up my writing God willing."[43] Since the manuscript is not extant, it is impossible to tell whether Lodge reconciled these contradictory impulses in his first novel.

Meanwhile, he experimented in other forms by writing a blank-verse drama, a farce, and the scenario for another play. "My farce will very likely appear in the autumn," he told his mother. "And if I squeeze my brains as dry as a withered lemon I shall, I will get another play on the stage by next year."[44] Despite his determination, all his winter projects failed; and Lodge's despondency was relieved only by his marriage during the summer of 1900.

The Davises had scheduled an extravagant social wedding for later summer at Bar Harbor, Maine; but the couple grew increasingly impatient with the preparations. Above all, Lodge and his bride wanted their wedding to have a spiritual dimension, and they could not reconcile their conviction with a "social" ceremony. At first, they decided to suffer through the Bar Harbor marriage as a formality and to arrange a private service afterwards. Then Elizabeth began to worry about the effect of the wedding on her father's poor health; and when Mrs. Davis started to complain of the bother and the expense of the affair, the couple took her at her word and eloped. They were secretly married at noon on August 18 in the Church of the Advent in Boston, which was empty except for Lodge's brother and a few worshipers.

During their extended honeymoon in Paris, Lodge resumed his

work in blank verse, the mode he would choose for his most ambitious poems; and he completed three verse tragedies, none of which proved to be publishable. In Paris, he also met George Gissing and was inspired by a reading of *New Grub Street* to write "Mediocracy." By 1901, Lodge's work in prose and drama was no longer motivated strictly by financial need, for Elizabeth received with her marriage an annuity that, combined with Lodge's annuity and his Senate salary, allowed the couple to live comfortably, if not luxuriously. Although he did not ignore the commercial possibilities of novels and plays, Lodge wrote primarily to establish a literary reputation that he feared could not be secured by poetry alone. Lodge never lost sight of his poetry, however; and, during the Parisian sojourn and under the influence of Swinburne and Whitman, he wrote most of what he would include in *Poems (1899–1902)*. He sold poems to the *Atlantic Monthly* and to the *Century*, in neither of which he had appeared, and to *Scribner's*. Self-mockingly, he wrote, "I suppose in time all this work will count and the world will appreciate my surpassing genius; just at present it doesn't seem to care a damn for me or my works. . . . Fortunately I am getting very calm about publishing and about the world generally."[45]

Henry Adams sensed that Lodge was rapidly growing conventional and urbane. Lodge had certainly matured considerably; and by the time of his return from Europe in September, 1901, he had adjusted to domestic responsibility, soon to be increased by the births of his three children: Henry Cabot (b. 1902), John Davis (b. 1903), and Helena (b. 1905). Yet his views remained iconoclastic enough to offend Edward Burlingame, who protested to Senator Lodge about one of Lodge's poems: "There are one or two passages . . . which I should doubt a little about printing in the Magazine for reasons which I must let Mr. Lodge think Philistine; but I am sincerely convinced that some obligations lie upon a magazine in this respect which would be ridiculous if applied to general literature or a book."[46] Paradoxically, Scribner's continued to publish Lodge's poems frequently in its magazine but never accepted another of his books.

In fact, Lodge could not find a reputable publisher for his second volume. At the suggestion of Charles Warren Stoddard, he sent both *Poems (1899–1902)* and "Mediocracy" to Will Clemens, a cousin of Mark Twain and a New York literary agent. Clemens failed to place "Mediocracy" but arranged a contract for *Poems* with

Cameron and Blake. "Clemens seems to think the volume will sell decently & is certainly giving it a first-rate advertisement," Lodge wrote hopefully.[47] Unfortunately, the publisher was financially unsound and went bankrupt in the midst of the press run for *Poems*. A very small edition appeared in late 1902 without supporting publicity.

Lodge sensed Walt Whitman's crucial importance for the future of American poetry, and *Poems* represented his attempt to mold his work to Whitman's example. He faithfully emulated Whitman's rhythms and buoyant mood; but, like Bliss Carmen and Richard Hovey in their Vagabondia phase, he produced only a weak echo of his model. Ignoring Whitman's hopes for a democratic American poetry, Lodge interpreted him as a prophet of Conservative Christian Anarchism—the elitist philosophy that Lodge and Henry Adams first formulated in 1896. In *Poems* and in his novels of this period, Lodge portrayed the Conservative Christian Anarchist for whom he would seek mythic prototypes in his later work.

CHAPTER 3

Conservative Christian Anarchism

IN the spring of 1896 in Paris, George Cabot Lodge and Trumbull Stickney with mock solemnity founded the Conservative Christian Anarchist party. More a playful intellectual pose than a rigorous philosophy, Conservative Christian Anarchism was designed, as Henry Adams put it, "to restore true poetry under the inspiration of the 'Götterdämmerung.' " When Stickney lost interest in the party, Lodge invited Adams to replace him. According to Adams, Conservative Christian Anarchism was based on a proper understanding of G. W. F. Hegel and Schopenhauer and upheld the "great principle of contradiction." Consequently, the party membership was limited to two.

Of course, no third member could be so much as considered, since the great principle of contradiction could be expressed only by opposites; and no agreement could be conceived, because anarchy, by definition, must be chaos and collision, as in the kinetic theory of a perfect gas. Doubtless this law of contradiction was itself agreement, a restriction of personal liberty inconsistent with freedom; but the "larger synthesis" admitted a limited agreement provided it were strictly confined to the end of larger contradiction. Thus the great end of all philosophy—the "larger synthesis"—was attained, but the process was arduous, and while Adams, as the older member, assumed to declare the principle, Bay Lodge necessarily denied both the assumption and the principle in order to assure its truth.[1]

As the whimsical tone of this passage implies, Adams to some extent regarded the "philosophy" of Conservative Christian Anarchism as a joke. Characteristically, however, Adams's sense of humor could be frivolous on one level but corrosively ironic on another. Conservative Christian Anarchism might be a joke, but it had a bitter punch line. "Here I am, today fifty-nine years old, and apparently in possession of my senses," Adams wrote to Lodge in 1897;

"yet my brain reels at the incredible chaos that I see around me wherever I look. Talk of anarchy! The whole world, politically, financially, socially, morally, artistically, economically, is one seething chaos which scares me to nervous prostration. I do sincerely believe that, for four years past, I have been the worst frightened man on earth, and to day I am more scared than ever."[2] Adams perceived the irony that modern society, terrified by the idea of political anarchism, was already anarchic.

In an anarchic world, only a philosophy of disorder could satisfy man's need of unity; therefore, Conservative Christian Anarchism could be taken seriously after all. The term itself manifested the "principle of contradiction," and Adams as Conservative Christian Anarchist could impose a philosophical order, however hypothetical, on chaos. Like his scientistic speculations in *The Rule of Phase Applied to History* and in *A Letter to American Teachers of History*, Adams's Conservative Christian Anarchism represented his desperate search for some "greater synthesis." This ultimate unity, however, had to be illusory because "in the last synthesis, order and anarchy were one, but . . . the unity was chaos."[3] Even if Conservative Christian Anarchism proved totally false as an interpretation of the multiverse, Adams considered a willed belief in it necessary to retain his sanity. It also supplied a locus of values in a world of moral relativity; for, as J. C. Levenson has said, "Adams accepted a world in which religion and society no longer provided sanctions for individual conduct. Within that world he chose, on his own responsibility, to conserve the liberal values among which he had lived for as long as he could remember and, ultimately, the Christian values of which he had acquired a personal memory after great pains."[4]

I *"Mediocracy"*

Lodge shared Adams's vision of a chaotic world; but, temperamentally incapable of Adams's resignation to the contradictions of life, Lodge redefined Conservative Christian Anarchism as a program of ethical rebellion. Adams postulated cosmic forces to explain the randomness of the multiverse, but Lodge blamed man and his society for the chaos of modern life. Although Adams came to see man as a dwarfed and impotent manikin whose destiny was blindly ordained by forces beyond his control and perhaps his understanding, Lodge asserted the power of the individual will (or soul) to shape its own destiny and to reclaim man's divine inheritance.

Using Conservative Christian Anarchism as both a rationale and a rationalization for his estrangement from society, Lodge transformed Adams's passive construct into a plan of action.

Lodge first formulated his theory of Conservative Christian Anarchism in "Mediocracy," the novel he began in 1901 under the influence of George Gissing's *New Grub Street*. Like Gissing's Edwin Reardon, Lodge's poet-protagonist Henry Everard revolts against the Grub Street literary world that has debased art into merchandise. Everard refuses to compromise with the commercial taste of society: "For his verse he had neither expected nor received more than a succès d'estime. The form was too perfect, the ideas too revolutionary to appeal to a commercial society whose God was order and who therefore hated genius as a form of moral and mental anarchy."[5]

An aristocrat by birth—Lodge always linked Conservative Christian Anarchism with an elite—Everard can afford to pursue "pure" art. Fearing the taint of money, Everard trusts his wife to handle his finances. Unfortunately, like Gissing's Amy Reardon, Alice Everard has been corrupted by the lust for affluence. She squanders her husband's money on luxuries and, in the face of enormous debts, realizes that she is too weak to bear poverty. Alice worships her husband's integrity too much to involve him in squalid financial problems; and, in attempting to solve them herself, she forms an adulterous liaison with wealthy but commonplace Arthur Creighton. Only after Creighton has corrupted Everard's wife and eloped with his daughter does Everard discover the calamity in his house. Shocked by his wife's betrayal, Everard decides, after rejecting suicide, to compromise his idealism by writing a "commercial" essay to pay the debts. "I am beaten," he moans as he burns the manuscript of his first novel, a denunciation of society to have been called "Mediocracy."

Regarded as fictionalized autobiography, "Mediocracy" illuminates Lodge's philosophy, for he used Everard as the exponent of his own anarchist doctrines. Lodge, as a Conservative Christian Anarchist, reacted against the assumptions of Social Darwinism; he rejected the identification of evolution with progress and the rationalization of ruthless business practices as the inevitable working-out of "natural selection." Lodge believed that Western culture had degenerated from a primitive state in which the individual intuited his potential for transcendence into a corrupt, commercial culture in which man's individuality and his sense of indwelling divinity had been lost. Since financial success, not mere survival, had become in modern culture the purpose of life, the "fittest," Lodge argued, were determined by economic and not natural criteria—by what he called "artificial selection." Artificial selection favored vulgarity over refinement, greed over charity, shrewdness over intelligence, deceit over honesty. In short, artificial selection bred a "Mediocracy." As Everard defines it in Lodge's novel,

There is no distinction left, no possibility of detecting the man of breeding from the general mass except the mere fact of the possession of wealth. . . . Distinctions are gone, consequently distinction is gone. There are no more classes, only masses, no more commoners and aristocrats, only a general level of mediocrity. And those who by their wealth and consequent leisure form a sort of lard on the rough, crude, greedy fabric of society, cannot form an aristocracy because the possibility of such a thing no longer exists, they are a mediocracy. (148–49)

The representative member of Mediocracy was the "Social or Conservative Man," who, while paying lip service to Christian values, based his "morality" on the commercial imperatives of society. Sacrificing even his identity for respectability, the "Conservative Man" became a shadow of his potentially divine primitive avatar.

Subject to mutation like the rest of nature, modern culture occasionally produced a sport. The "Eccentric or Anarchist," a reversion to the primitive type, instinctively revolted against the respectable artifice of society. Because he was fully "human," the anarchist sensed his transcendent potential; he felt compelled to assert it in the role of "Truth Seer and Teller"; and the cost of speaking the "Truth" was alienation. Everard muses to himself in the opening pages of "Mediocracy": "It seemed to him that in the world's mediocrity, in the lower middle-class state of mind of society, there existed no atmosphere of opinion in which his own judgments could find comparison. If he went into the world he was like a man with a voice in a place where no sound-transferring medium existed. The world as he found it, the world of this stock-market civilization, was deaf to him, or he mute for it,—at any rate they had no common speech" (10–11). The anarchist recognized "Truth" in the teachings of the wisest men: Buddha, Socrates, Jesus. Since the "True" values were also the oldest values and since, in Western culture, they had long been associated with Jesus, the anarchist paradoxically became a "conservative" and a "Christian."

The Conservative Christian Anarchist knew that his revolt must lead to exile from and eventual destruction by society, which would recognize him as a threat to the established order. As Everard explains,

The modern world is essentially practical. Physically it is centralized, coherent and of unreal power. Spiritually and mentally it is anarchic, disrupted, futile. Therefore the work of the world needs practical men. . . . The Idealist is useless—or worse. Now conceive of some poor devil who is put into Harvard ignorant of these facts. He becomes acquainted with pure ideas, with sentiments, imagination—poetry. Suppose he takes them seriously, suppose he comes to spiritual reality and being of honest mind determines to apply practically to life the teachings of Christ or Plato, or any other Idealist? What happens? Two things. He is opposing society as he finds it in its most fundamental basic principles and he is crushed. So much for the Individual. But multiply him by thousands and you form the nucleus of an anarchic and disorganizing force in the very centre of the Social Fabric. (36)

By such martyrdom, the anarchist hoped to arouse the "humanity" of other malcontents—ones previously cowed into submission by society. Because of the advanced state of human degeneration, only a few—in effect, an elite—could heed the prophecy of the anarchist; but these few would perhaps form the nucleus of a new society to be founded on the principle of human divinity.

It must be stressed that Lodge's Conservative Christian Anarchism was an aesthetic and ethical but *not* a political philosophy. In fact, Lodge apparently never considered the political implications of his ideas. He felt a kinship with political anarchists so far as he could sympathize with their ethical aims. In 1905, he published a sonnet to Maxim Gorky, which his father later omitted from Lodge's complete works:

> My love is with thee and with Liberty!
> The self-same human offal,—Czar and priest,
>   Coward and liar, idiot and beast,—
>   The self-same men slew Jesus who slay thee!
> But now, despite their sly ferocity,
>   The hounds of justice by thy hand released
>   Howl in the swinish middle of their feast,
>   And fear appals them of their destiny!
> For we, Lovers and Liberators, we,
>   God-less and law-less Saviours who reclaim

Men from the reverence of power and name,—
In the dark places of Humanity,
We light a conflagration whose blind flame
Roars in the ears of them who butcher thee![6]

Although Lodge spoke recklessly of "conflagration," he advocated
not political upheaval but Nietzschean transvaluation. The ultimate
victory of Conservative Christian Anarchism would result not from
mass revolution but from the evolution of "True" values among an
elite. Lodge feared that political anarchism would reduce art to the
least common denominator of the "mass with purely reactive mental
processes."[7] A mass society would be worse than Mediocracy. If
bourgeois society ostracized the anarchist, it at least allowed him the
freedom of his alienation and provided an order, however artificial,
necessary for the existence of art.

Michael Wreszin has argued that an antipolitical, elitist, anarchist
tradition in America can be traced to Transcendentalism. "The
anarchist impulse found in Thoreau, Emerson, some of the Tran-
scendentalists and abolitionists was antipolitical to the core and often
antidemocratic. . . . In America anarchism may be the only logical
refuge for the aspiring aristocrat."[8] In Lodge's case, Conservative
Christian Anarchism seemed to be the only logical refuge for an
aspiring Brahmin in the midst of Mediocracy.

II   "The Genius of the Commonplace"

Although Lodge deplored Boston's degeneration into a "Banker's
world," he regarded New York "society" as the center of American
Mediocracy. "O lord I don't like New York," he wrote to his mother
during a visit there. "Money money money—it smells in the
Streets[.] It's pure plutocracy & we are the hangers-on—unless
we're anarchists."[9] Lodge depicted the rise and fall of a New York
plutocrat in his second novel, "The Genius of the Commonplace,"
written during 1902.

The novel opens at the New York Stock Exchange. Lanthorpe, a
Socialist, and Verdren, a Darwinist, survey with analytical fascination the "sea of faces fiercely contracted with an expression of angry
ferocity, a forest of right arms describing gestures of the most appalling violence, a tempest of voices crying out enigmatic names and
numbers with inconceivable loudness."[10] In the crowd, Verdren
spies Nicolas Crannard, a man he knew briefly as a child, who is on

the threshold of a spectacular career in New York finance. Crannard, Lodge's protagonist, is the antithesis of Henry Everard. As a
child, Crannard was indoctrinated by his father with the idea that
"life was divided into two things, work and amusement, work, the
making of money, and amusement, the spending of money. There
was nothing else" (20). Furthermore, Crannard has been taught that
the only significant failure in life is the failure to make money. Thus
when his own father was ruined by speculation, Crannard mercilessly condemned him and drove him to suicide.

Lodge wrote to Adams in 1900, "I guess money-making is a pure
instinct unconnected in any way with the reason, but to be
Schopenhauerian, a direct & immediate faculty of the understanding."[11] Crannard manifests the highest development of the instinct
of money-making. Shrewd, brutal, and unscrupulous, he prefigures
such titanic financiers as Frank Norris's Curtis Jadwin and Theodore Dreiser's Frank Cowperwood. Crannard is the "genius of the
commonplace" because he can manipulate society's ethics to his
own advantage. "Crannard was the direct result of competition,"
Lanthorpe remarks. "He was a man of very superior force and nothing more. He had neither aim, guidance nor principles of his own.
Society supplied him with all three!—Money for an aim, competition for guidance and for principles the usual stale old formulas of
conduct. The aim he accepted and the guidance; but he was a man of
superior force, and that force gave him the practical veracity to
disregard society's ready-made principles and frankly take for his
morals expediency" (182–83).

Crannard's expediency is dramatized in the first chapter when
Severn, the man who gave Crannard his start in New York, drops
dead on the floor of the Stock Exchange. While the crowd mills
about in confusion, Crannard literally leaps over Severn's body to
sell his list short before news of Severn's death can drive prices
down. Later, when Crannard's enemies in the stock market try to
ruin him, expediency demands an adulterous relationship with
Grace Arenton, who owns the stock he needs to cover his buying on
margin. The bored, rich wife of a "society" dullard, Grace Arenton
is attracted to Crannard by his crude sexual force, and she willingly
becomes his dupe. When rumor of their affair—which, in fact, has
never been consummated—threatens Crannard's improving social
status, Crannard cruelly deserts Grace and cynically saves himself
by marrying Bertha Alisford, a vacant-headed but socially unassail-

able debutante. By the end of the novel, Crannard has not only acquired a fortune, but has also bullied his way into exclusive New York "society."

The key to his success, as he brags to Verdren, has been his perception that the standards and principles of society are "nothing but the world's timidities deified, Gods of sawdust, bogeys, shadows!" (173). In other words, Crannard achieves the insight of all Lodge's Conservative Christian Anarchists into the hypocrisy of modern society. On his wedding day, Crannard smugly surveys the scene of his triumph:

> He saw the grave and dignified Bishop close beside him before the altar; he saw Alisford and his daughter . . . walking to the slow rhythm of the familiar march; he saw the well-filled pews, row on row of clean and correct men, of women in gay hats and bright spring dresses, all of wealth, respectability and fashion, standing silent and attentive to behold the completion of his triumph. . . . It rejoiced him that God and society, religion and respectability should combine to sanction his life and acts, and certainly this temple of pompous hypocrisies, worldly conservatism and meaningless traditions was the exactly appropriate place for such a ceremony, for was not this church, this pageant, this mummery conserved for the sole purpose of dispensing to those very deeds which Christ had most deplored, to the self-same men whom Christ had denounced until they caused his death, the sanction of his portentous name? (175–76)

But because Crannard has channeled all his life-force into money-making, he never discovers the spiritual dimension in his anarchism. At all his moments of crisis in the novel, Crannard is haunted by a nightmare vision: "Down before his eyes, in a blinding torrent rained the abbreviations and numbers of the stock list, thro' his vision whirled the endless white ribbon of the ticker, in his ears thundered the high, fierce roar of the Stock Exchange" (180). Literally blinded and deafened by his materialism, Crannard is a Conservative Christian Anarchist *manqué*, a benighted brother to Henry Everard. Crannard unleashes the destructive force of his inner energy, but the result is not redemption but damnation. Crannard is damned, finally, because he assumes that everyone he manipulates is powerless to resist. As Verdren warns him,

> You are like a man who counts on everyone playing the game according to rules and then wins by breaking the rules himself. . . . Obviously you must win. But I warn you! It's not entirely safe to base one's whole life on the

supposition that no one else will perceive that the rules are merely formulas devoid of importance. Someone always may, you always risk being attacked by sheer reality, and you know yourself how powerless are all conventions and morals, all the safeguards of your life, in short, against such an attack, for it is precisely by such unlawful warfare that you have won success. (174–75

The agent of Crannard's downfall, ironically, is hapless Dudley Arenton. By using Grace Arenton, Crannard has unwittingly undermined her allegiance to respectability. According to Lodge, once "Truth" has been revealed, either prophetically by a Henry Everard or inadvertently by a Nicolas Crannard, liberation inevitably follows. Thus, Grace declares independence from her meaningless marriage. Dudley, whose chief worry in life is the menu at his club, cannot bear to see his stable world collapse under the force of his wife's defiant admission of adultery. Driven to madness, Dudley reverts to animalism and clubs Crannard to death as he escorts his bride from the church.

Whereas Crannard is the anarchist *manqué,* Dudley represents the mass of men whose lives are so stunted that "Truth" can bring only derangement. On the day of the murder, Dudley, in a daze, wanders into the zoo. As he passes the animal cages, he is struck by "a sudden realization that he and they shared the self-same life. . . . In reality then he was merely an animal! The ruined stronghold of his life-long prejudices offered no resistance to this subversive thought and he accepted it without pleasure or repulsion" (177). Dudley believes that he is no more than an animal because he is incapable of seeing that he is potentially divine.

This insight, reserved for Lodge's elite, is achieved in the novel by Grace Arenton. Aroused by Crannard's sexuality, Grace progresses from feeling new sexual depths in herself to an intuition of her spiritual depths. At the end, she has begun the search for the "soul's inheritance" that all Lodge's Conservative Christian Anarchists must make. "You see I don't know what anything means to me,—even life itself," Grace says. "I have everything to examine, to discover, to think out for myself. Really, I began to live only a few weeks ago" (182). Lodge implies that Grace will eventually become a full-fledged anarchist like Henry Everard or Edward Crawley, the Poet and the Artist, respectively, who move through the novel in counterpoint to the corrupt and hollow people of New York "society." Everard and Crawley are authentic anarchists because they perceive the whole "Truth." As Everard defines it, "Truth is the direct personal apprehension, unhindered by cowardice, prejudice or interest, of the content of experience, whether physical, intellectual or spiritual. Inevitably, therefore, Truth has as many degrees as there are individuals" (184).

"Truth" for Lodge finds its highest expression in art. Thus Everard and Crawley are distinguished from the "society" characters by their superior taste, just as they are from the doctrinaire characters by their refusal to systematize reality. Verdren, the scientist, and Lanthorpe, the ideologue, ignore the individual nature of "Truth" by trying to impose their narrowly conceived theories on the world. Verdren's Social Darwinism sees the struggle for survival only in animal terms of superior strength; Lanthorpe proposes only to change the political system, not to change the underlying values of society. The true anarchist, as Everard says, seeks "to destroy forms and systems and sciences": "For Truth is not a thing that can be given and received. It lies about us all, close and plentiful and limitless as the air of heaven, and we live in a vacuum surrounded by the glass of lies. No one can do more than destroy, break the glass and let in the air. That is what the Truth-seers and Truth-tellers from Christ to Whitman have done in the past and in the future they will do the same" (185–86).

Encouraged by Stoddard to publish his novel, Lodge first sent the manuscript of "The Genius of the Commonplace" to Henry Adams. In an embarrassed letter, Adams finally suggested after pages of tactful circumlocution that Lodge should "lock up the volume for a year. Then read it over—carefully—and tell me your conclusion." Although Adams admired the youthful exuberance of Lodge's novel, he objected both to its subject—"The New Yorker bores me in real life; how can he amuse me in fiction?"—and to its moralistic tone.[12] Lodge agreed that the novel contained more "commentary" than "art," and he concluded that "the vice is too ingrained to be eradicated."[13] Although he vowed to write another novel to correct the defects of "The Genius of the Commonplace," Lodge turned his energies exclusively to poetry after 1902.

Unquestionably, "The Genius of the Commonplace" has its defects; it tends toward both melodrama and diatribe. But this novel, a distinct improvement over "Mediocracy" in style and fictional sophistication, is more than a tract for Conservative Christian Anarchism. It is also a competent and absorbing novel in its own right and a suggestive literary-historical document. In his portrait of Nicolas Crannard, Lodge added notably to the gallery of business titans in the American economic novel from Howells' *The Landlord at Lion's Head* to Norris's *The Octopus* and *The Pit* to Dreiser's Cowperwood trilogy. Furthermore, in Lodge's depiction of the decay of New York "society" through materialism, he anticipated such novels of manners as Wharton's *The House of Mirth* and *The Age of Innocence* and F. Scott Fitzgerald's *The Beautiful and Damned* and *The Great Gatsby*.

III Poems (1899–1902)

Conservative Christian Anarchism informed Lodge's conception of poetry as well as of fiction. He envisioned "The Poet" as a prophet-seer who chanted the "Truth" to an indifferent or hostile society. "The Poet" was not a representative man but an alienated elitist:

> He comes last of the long processional,
> Last of the perfect lovers, doomed as they
> To live ever more lonely day by day
> By all rejected and condemned by all.
> (I, 159)

Although Emerson and Whitman would have repudiated this view, some of their work—especially "Self-Reliance," "The Poet," and "Preface" to 1855 *Leaves of Grass*—invited such a misinterpretation. Thus, despite Whitman's insistent warnings that a poet detached from the democratic en-masse would fail, Lodge cast Whitman himself as the model of the alienated poet.

Lodge considered *Leaves of Grass*, his own copy of which was dilapidated from use and filled with marginalia, almost literally sacred writ. As early as 1898, Lodge was quoting Whitman in his letters to support his own anarchist views. He placed Whitman in a line of "Truth Seers and Tellers" that had included Leopardi, Browning, Leconte de Lisle, and Swinburne. Lodge intended to commemorate these poet-heroes in a long poem to be called "Servae Laudes," and he completed the sections on Leopardi and Whitman.

Lodge thought the key to understanding Whitman's poetry was careful attention to rhythm. After scanning dozens of poems, he concluded that Whitman habitually used particular rhythms for particular kinds of poems—for what Lodge called "lyrics," "panoramas," and "reflective poems." In the long poems Lodge detected a symphonic structure, related to musical modulations in rhythm. He wrote in the margin next to "Salut au Monde":

This poem I *think* I understand in its musical conception & have intelligently interpreted perhaps. . . . The poems must be considered first as pure music, the words void of concrete thought as the notes of a violin. Then after this basis is understood the thought in its R[hythmic] connection must be studied. The great pt. is the R[hythmic] *totality*. Cf. each poem as compared to a poem of Shelley's for instance. There is the same musical difference as between Siegfried & the Zauberflote—the first being a R[hythmic] & musical totality each part existent for the other parts & all coordinate & the second merely a compilation of independent melodies written on formal lines.[14]

Lodge diligently analyzed what he called the "rhythms" and "counter-rhythms" of such poems as "When Lilacs Last in the Dooryard Bloom'd" and "Passage to India," and he noted a correlation between changes in rhythm and shifts in tone or theme.

By focusing on rhythm in *Leaves of Grass*, Lodge failed to grasp the importance of Whitman's language. In the Whitman section of "Servae Laudes," Lodge combined a mechanical imitation of Whitman's rhythms with his own inflated diction; the result was almost a parody of the original:

> Passage to more than India, O my soul,
> Passage to suns and systems, seas and streams,
> Forest and fields—My land and all I love.
> Passage, swift passage to myself, to God—
> Immediate passage! Are my lovers there?
> Are theirs the arms to cover, the hearts to pray?
> Passage to more than India—O make haste!
> Soul shall interpret, I am plumed for flight!
> Passage and change from love to all I love
> Safe with the perfect comrade—I shall pass
> And cease my singing, as I change to song.[15]

Lodge showed the Whitman section to fellow Whitman admirer Charles Warren Stoddard, who dissuaded him from trying to publish it. Undaunted by Stoddard's warning that Whitman's style is not easily imitated, Lodge launched into a Conservative Christian Anarchist's version of *Leaves of Grass*—his *Poems (1899–1902)*. Dedicated to Whitman, the volume borrowed as liberally from Swinburne. Unfortunately, most of the poems were as weak as "Servae Laudes"; and one reviewer was provoked to complain that "Mr. Lodge simply echoes either Whitman or Swinburne until the reader is ready to call out a plague on both."[16]

With few exceptions—"The Greek Galley," "Day and Dark," and some of the sonnets—the poems are failures. At his worst, Lodge, intent on translating his ideas into verse, smothered his philosophy in a fog of anapests which, as in Swinburne's poetry, lull the reader into disregard for meaning. Even the partially successful poems suffered from Lodge's adherence to genteel poetics.

For Lodge, clarity of expression varied directly with strictness of form, and the sonnets and disciplined lyrics of *Poems* succeed far better than the poems in anapests or blank verse. One may compare, for example, these parallel lines from, first, "The Greek Galley" and, second, "The Passage":

> The sound of the sea, the sway of the song, the swing of the oar!
>   Out of the darkness, over the naked seas,
>   Our galley is come
>   With a shiver and leap,
>   As the blade bites deep
>   To the sway of back and the bend of knees,
>   As she drives for home
>   Out of the darkness, over the naked seas,
> To the sound of sea and the sway of song and the sweep of oar!
>
> (I, 126)

> Onward ever and outward ever, over the uttermost verge of the sea,
> Out over the tremulous tides and the trackless waste ways to the wall of the
>   firmament free,
> Fulfilled of the light of ineffable spaces, the echoless thunder of wind in the
>   night,
> And broad in the burnished blue hollow of heaven the endless procession of
>   darkness and light.
>
> (I, 144)

In both poems Lodge used the metaphor of the journey of the soul as a voyage. In "The Greek Galley," he achieved relative economy of language, visual imagery, and an effectively syncopated rhythm.

In "The Passage," however, for the sake of rhythm and alliteration, Lodge padded his lines with nebulous adjectives: "uttermost," "tremulous," "trackless," "ineffable" (a Lodge favorite), "echoless," "burnished." Aural rather than visual in its effect, "The Passage" diffuses the spirited movement of "The Greek Galley" and blurs its meaning.

Lodge imitated *Leaves of Grass* by dividing *Poems* into thematic sections that trace the progress of the soul. In "Outward!," the first section, Lodge celebrates the awakening of the transcendental impulse in part through awareness of nature.

So it ends! I reaped the harvest, lived the long and lavish day,
Saw the earliest sunlight shiver thro' the breakers' endless play,
Felt the noonday's warm abundance, shared the hours of large repose,
While the stately sun descended thro' the twilight's sumptuous close.

Now the night-fall— Ah! I guess the immortal secret, glimpse the goal,
Know the hours have scanted nothing, know each fragment hints the whole,
While the Soul in power and freedom dares and wills to claim its own,
Star over star, a larger, lovelier unknown heaven beyond the known!
                                                        (I, 147–48)

Several poems in this section, such as "A Song For Revolution," depict the artificial culture that the soul must reject; but, when Lodge tried to describe the soul's "heritage," he relied on the vague power of aureate words to suggest what he could not make concrete.

The second section, "For E. L.," inspired by his wife, argues that, even more than in nature, the soul intuits transcendence through human love. Lodge envisions the female *persona* of the section as the supreme consoler:

She, child of mightier days and larger loves,
    Stands like a silence in the sound of life,
    And recent things about her beauty seem
Vain and unlovely as our human strife;
    Wise and ineffable as Truth She moves
    As moves a great thought thro' a foolish dream.
                                                        (I, 171)

Like Henry Adams's Virgin of Chartres, "E. L." offers to the soul, battered and tossed by its voyage, a peaceful harbor:

Pour down thy hair between the world and me!
Between myself and my exhausted soul
Spread, in the dreadful vistas where my goal
Saddens and fails, thy love's euthanasy!
Fold me away from Time and let me be
Silent and ceased from bitterness, be thou
Tacit as childhood and thine ivory brow
Thoughtless, and be thou tender utterly!
Strength, give me strength to spare the futile tears!
Give me the consciousness of something proved:
Faith, wisdom, personal and briefly true.
I sift the scant, earned knowledge of my years
Like dust between my hands, and all I loved
And hoped and dreamed dissolves and blends to you!
                                              (I, 173–74)

Conservative Christian Anarchism expressed the side of Lodge
committed to battle society, and for Lodge, as Conservative Christian Anarchist, "love's euthanasy" presented grave dangers. Love of
woman shields the anarchist from the world and saps the strength
needed to sustain his moral combat. Love of woman also tempts the
anarchist to mistake the sweet but temporal pleasure of sex for the
immortal joy he can find only in transcendence. For Schopenhauer,
subjugation of the Will necessitated an ascetic life. Lodge, like
Nietzsche, inverted Schopenhauer's pessimism but retained his as-
ceticism. The soul (or Will) must be allowed its full expansion to
human divinity, but transcendence requires the severing of all
human attachments, even to woman.

Woman as Circe is the theme of "Ishtar," the third section of
Poems. Invoking the myth of Tännhauser and Venus, Lodge warns
that love of woman can enslave the soul by distracting it from its
journey outward. Ishtar (Venus) proclaims the power of procreative
love:

For me, the eldest and the loveliest God,
For me and for my equal happiness
The woman aches with sweet maternal stress,
The slow seed breaks beneath the reeking sod.
For me the strong, swift feet of dawn are shod
With fire, for me the flowers' frail petals press
Fearless and faithful, and warm winds caress

> The violet sea-ways where of old I trod.
> For me the long, resounding years return
> With gradual seasons, and the stately sun
> Shepherds thro' void infinity his brood;
> And only thro' my knowledge man may turn,
> To larger consciousness the soul has won,
> Leaving his outworn body for my food.
>
> (I, 187)

Ensnared at first by Ishtar, Tännhauser finally challenges her and declares his dedication to the quest:

> Not thine the power! I go from thee to me!
> Mine is the task—to teach my human soul
> The vastness of the immortal mood and thus
> Lift my fierce life to immortality!
>
> (I, 196)

Tännhauser, speaking for Lodge, explicitly forsakes woman as a shield between the anarchist and the world. Paradoxically, to become fully "human"—that is, divine—the anarchist must purge himself of the tenderest of human feelings: for woman and home. In fact, the superhuman behavior of the anarchist in the transcendent state may appear inhuman by earthly standards. Lodge would amplify these themes in *Cain* and *Herakles*. Lodge did not restrict transcendence to men—witness Grace Arenton and Eve— but he believed that women were more likely than men to sacrifice the divine possibility for the certainty of human passion.

In "Variations," the fourth section, Lodge considers death as the ultimate transcendence, as the gateway to immortality and peace:

> Hush child! Be still and give thy fingers rest,
> 　Thine eyes the darkness, and thy lips that press
> Hard on the lips of life with fierce caress,
> 　Ease from their hunger and thy guideless quest.
> Ask of the vacant eyes and stirless breast
> 　Of life's last angel, pale Forgetfulness,
> Peace, and release from thought's eternal stress:
> 　She, of life's violent, fervent Gods, is best.
> Peace, child! Beneath her hand the fretful flame
> 　Of long desire grows frail and faint as dream:
> The immediate life is alien to despair.

> Held on her heart seem life and death the same.
> And nothing is at all and all things seem,
> And if life dies thou shalt not even care!
>
> (I, 204)

Lodge envisions death in Neo-Platonic or Buddhist terms as a reunion with the Primal Force of the universe in which all contradictions are merged into Oneness:

> Thou must forget or else 't were vain to die,
> Death with thy memories is not death at all;
> Passion and pain and pleasure, thou and I,
> Life and its longings, must, beyond recall,
> Cease or unite or merge and death must come
> Like seaward wind that takes the rain-drop home.
>
> Death shall forget tho' life's immortal power
> That gave thee strength to bear thy human fate
> Suffer and strive. Thro' death the mystic flower
> Of soul expands until thy youth's wise hate
> Of life has utterly passed in love away,
> While death prepares the spiritual day.
>
> (I, 207)

The final section of *Poems* comprises a single long poem, "The Song of Man," which Lodge meant to summarize his volume. The speaker recounts the steps of the soul's journey from rebellion against society through rejection of old religions through the temptations of Ishtar to the ultimate realization of self-divinity:

> "For my God is the friend that I cherish, and my God is the woman I love,
> My God is the Spring on the hillsides, the Sea and the marvel thereof,
> My God is the justice of sunlight unhindered by power or pelf,
> And vast beyond all and inclusive of all things, my God is Myself!"
>
> (I, 227)

Although Lodge derived this notion in part from Schopenhauer and Nietzsche, and in part from Bigelow's Buddhism, his belief in the potential divinity of man in an American context can be described as literalized Transcendentalism. As Frederick Conner has said, Transcendentalism was " 'radical subjectivism,' resting on the belief that the 'I' is the only immediately experienced reality and that the objects of knowledge are known only as the contents of consciousness." The Transcendentalist could postulate an Oversoul as the ultimate cause of his progression from the plane of natural facts to that of spiritual facts, but the transcendental feeling could be experienced only subjectively. One logical conclusion was that the "I" itself contained the energy for transcendence. "Thus, no matter how he may palliate the fact by the use of traditional theological terminology or how much it may be actually extenuated by the persistence of traditional religious attitudes, the god of the transcendentalist is simply himself writ large. Lodge . . . simply made this plainer than the others, deliberately rejecting the palliations to which many clung."[17]

This literalized Transcendental doctrine became the persistent theme of Lodge's work after 1900. Lodge experimented with different forms and genres to explore different facets of his philosophy, but he returned always to the idea: "And vast beyond all and inclusive of all things, my God is Myself!"

CHAPTER 4

Sons of Man

BY 1901, Lodge's intellectual development had reached maturity, and he began in a variety of forms to reiterate the doctrines of Conservative Christian Anarchism. Implicit in Lodge's philosophy was a tension between domestic life and the imaginative life of the poet-seer. Lodge believed that "Truth" destroyed every conventional institution, including the family; and in *Cain*, his first published verse-drama, he presented an archetypal family disintegration.

Lodge's use of dramatic form in *Cain* reflected the influence of Langdon Mitchell, to whom Lodge was introduced during the winter of 1902–03. Eleven years older than Lodge, Mitchell at first assumed the role of Lodge's literary mentor; and, after Trumbull Stickney's death in 1904, Mitchell became Lodge's closest friend. The son of the popular novelist and psychiatrist S. Weir Mitchell, Langdon Mitchell has been remembered, if at all, as the author of *The New York Idea*, a satire of marital mores in New York "society" that tickled Broadway audiences in 1905. Except for *Becky Sharp*, his adaptation of *Vanity Fair*, which was performed in New York in 1899 and 1900, Mitchell's plays had earned him little reputation at the time he first met Lodge.

As with Stickney, Lodge shared many literary and philosophical notions with Mitchell. In 1903, during a visit to Tuckernuck Island, the two men read each other's poetry and, over bottles of wine, talked far into the night about literature and religion; a recurrent topic was the significance of Jesus and his teachings. Since Lodge's days at Harvard, when he had written a term paper on Ernest Renan, Lodge had held a detheologized view of Jesus as a man who seemed divine because he was fully human. In other words, Lodge interpreted Jesus as a Conservative Christian Anarchist. Edward Crawley, Henry Everard's friend in Lodge's novels, prizes above all his work a painting of "Christ at the moment when he called to God that he had forsaken him, Christ straining forward from the cross, his muscles drawn with terrible effort, his face awful with a sudden and portentous despair. But Crawley had caused to shine thro' the haggard agony of the Galilean's ascetic face the light of all his so measureless tenderness and the dawn, as it were, of the greater light of a last and more complete revelation."[1] What Jesus had realized in his last moments of life was that, since God had indeed forsaken him, human divinity must result from the expansion of the soul to the limits of consciousness. Like Nietzsche, Lodge regarded belief in the Christian God to be a superstition of slaves and children and the established church to be a tool of society for obscuring the "Truth."

Such thoughts informed Lodge's dedication of *Cain:* "To the deathless memory of JESUS OF NAZARETH seer and sayer of truth who was believed only by the poor and outcast, who was recognized by all reputable and respectable people as the avowed enemy of law, order and religion, and who was at last brought to his death by the priesthood of the orthodox church through the operation of the established courts of social justice, this poem is inscribed with measureless love" (I, 231). Determined to save the "Truth" of Biblical myth from the distortions of the church, Lodge in *Cain* deliberately inverted the orthodox reading of Genesis 4.

1 Cain: A Drama

From the sparse details of the story of Cain and Abel in the Bible, Lodge extrapolated his three-act, blank-verse drama. In Act I, Lodge dramatized his vision of the aftermath of Adam's and Eve's expulsion from the Garden. Adam is repentant, but Eve is secretly defiant; and these attitudes are echoed in those of their children, who offer their sacrifices to God in Act II. After the offering of the rebellious Cain is rejected by God, he kills his brother Abel, not out of wrath so much as out of a desire to exterminate Abel's servile attitude. Cursed and exiled by God, Cain in Act III undertakes Lodge's archetypal journey of human transcendence. Cain makes, as Adams put it, "the superhuman effort of lifting himself and the universe by sacrifice, and, of course, by destroying the attachments which are most vital, in order to attain."[2] In short, *Cain* transformed the ideas of Conservative Christian Anarchism into myth.

With the maturation of Lodge's philosophy, he sought an effective literary vehicle. His efforts in the novel had produced fictionalized philosophical symposia in which characters served as mouthpieces for various positions. Lodge hoped the mythic verse-drama, traditionally used for themes of cosmic dimensions, would allow a more dramatic and intense statement of philosophical ideas. To give his theme the most elevated presentation, Lodge eliminated all superfluities of plot, character, and scene. Using the Bible as his text and confining himself to four characters, Lodge tried to emulate the starkness of Greek tragedy. Adams believed that Lodge had more aptitude for dramatic than for lyric poetry, and the mythic verse-drama had a distinct formal advantage. In *Cain* and *Herakles*, the psychology and symbolic actions of the characters compensate for the lack of concrete metaphors, which Lodge's nonvisual imagination failed to generate. His verse-dramas also shared the paradoxical quality of his lyrics—that what the hero must reject is more clearly depicted than what he seeks. Thus in *Cain* the servile characters Adam and Abel speak better poetry than Eve and Cain, and in *Herakles* Creon virtually preempts the poem from Herakles.

At the opening of *Cain*, Adam wakes from a nightmare of his temptation in the Garden; and, like a whining child, he clings to Eve for support and consolation:

> Visions! Visions!—O shield me, take my hands!
> Let my face lie against thy breast a while—
> I dreamed of Paradise and God—no more,
> No more! I am too shaken utterly!
> Vague am I, vague and desolate as mist!
> My soul suffers—O heart, how sad it is!
> Life is too tragic of its memories—
> Hold me—I need thy tenderness, I need
> Thy calm and pitiful hands to comfort me.
>   (I, 238)

Rejecting the "perishable joys" of life outside Eden, Adam can justify his suffering only through "dumb obedience to the will of God":

> Nay!—tho' my life is bruised with sore affliction
> And dire repentance blasts my happiness,
> Tho' in remembrance Paradise forever
> Blooms with fresh light and flowers ineffable,

> Clear pieties and peaceful innocence,
> Against the gloom of this grieved sentience
> Of violence and starvation, yet I bear,
> Scornful of tears, the grief and scorn of life!
> Faith is the stern, austere acknowledgment
> And dumb obedience to the will of God:
> Such faith my soul has kept inviolable!
> What tho' He crush me, is He not the Lord!
>
> (I, 250–51)

From Eve's first speech, however, it is clear that she shares neither her husband's self-pity nor his submissiveness. She delights in the power of life itself, as manifested in the abundance and beauty of nature:

> The rapt silence! The dark twilight!—It dawns!
> The multitude of the ineffable stars
> That lamped the viewless parapets of heaven,
> Melt in the light like pearls in golden wine;
> The void globe of the calm firmament
> Glows; the immemorable ecstasy
> Thrills in the vital fabric of creation,
> And—hark!—a bird wakes somewhere in the world!
> Somewhere a burst seed splits the naked sod,
> Somewhere a flower folded at evening
> Petal by petal bares its inmost heart
> In perfect trust and drinks the dewfall! —Life,
> O Life, imperishable and resistless! Life,
> Fragile as joy and free as destiny!
> O breath of life tender and passionate,
> Sweet breath of sap and imminent foliage
> Blown thro' the level ether and low light!
>
> (I, 235–36)

Eve believes that fallen man has entered the continuity of nature and thereby become heir to its pains and joys:

> Now are we not withholden by God's grace
> From all mortality; we know at last
> How we are fashioned of the selfsame clay
> Whence his creative hands divinely shaped

Behemoth and the bird of paradise.
On the bare uplands of reality
Our feet walk level with the whole of life!
Therefore the tender and impermanent joys,
The warm, frail happiness of mortal things
Are ours at last, our earned inheritance.
                                                    (I, 241)

By placing her faith in the life force instead of in God, Eve can
envision a naturalistic immortality:

Is death a silence so eventual?
It cannot be! If life must find a term
Vain is the passionate utterance of life,
Vain the sore travail in which my womb conceived
The stalwart children of thy generation!
It cannot be! What tho' the hand of death
Shall smite my mouth with silence utterly
And feed spring flowers of my carrion?
Yet is eternity within me!—Hark!
Whispers, whispers of immortality!
As it were a shell found inland, so is life
Fulfilled with murmurs of an infinite sea!
                                                    (I, 245)

Although Eve suspects that God's power is illusory, she does not
challenge it at first, preferring a kind of silent agnosticism. Cain,
however, openly repudiates his father's faith; and Act I ends with a
quarrel between Cain and Adam over Cain's "impiety." Eve, who
secretly takes her elder son's side, tries unsuccessfully to intercede.

In Act II, Cain and Abel reenact the conflict of beliefs in which
their parents had obliquely engaged. Like his mother (and
Wordsworth), Cain hears "whispers of immortality" in the grandeur
of nature:

Tacit and distant as life's thought of death
Earth lies beneath me patterned with sheer hills,
Deserts and forest-marches, flashing streams
And sea-scapes vast beyond the power of vision.
. . . .
As one sequestered in the tower of thought

> I stand aloof from restless strife and sound,
> Withdrawn beyond the fellowship of life.
> Solitude, silence and tranquillity,
> Immensity of elemental things,—
> Haply in you at last the soul finds room,
> And liberty and light haply in you!
>
> (I, 266–67)

Like his father, Abel meekly bows to the will of God:

> I put no trust in strength or youth,
>   Or power, or thought, or mighty deeds;
>   I ask of life no more than needs;
> I know but this— Thy will is Truth!
>
> (I, 269)

When Cain's sacrifice is rejected by God, he suddenly realizes what his mother has not yet discovered: that the transcendental force he has experienced in nature emanates not from God but from his own soul. Cain recognizes that God is merely the anthropomorphization of human fears:

> God is not liberty but law, not love
> But mercy, not redemption but despair;
> Not joy but lethargy and meek content,
> Not grief's robust acknowledgment of wrong
> But abject lamentation and remorse,
> Not justice but forgiveness or revenge,
> Not strength but safety, not the change of growth,
> Fluid unrest of free development,
> But rules and customs and establishments,
> Limits and lies—the servitude of man!
> So even is God and God's significance!
> But Lo! at last man wakes and stands and strives!
> Liberty!—Light!—Thy deed was not in vain,
> Mother! Thy womb has not engendered slaves!
>
> (I, 290–91)

Echoing the words of Jesus, whom he prefigures, Cain desperately tries to convert his brother:

Turn from thy cowardice and childish fears!
For whosoever will save his life shall lose it;
But whosoever shall lose his life for truth
And liberty, the same shall save his life!
What shall it profit thee if thy life is gained
And all the splendour of all the world beside
If soul is lost? What shall it profit thee
To live sheltered in comfort and content,
If thou must yield the soul's inheritance
To alien government and forego thy crown,
Forfeit thy power and pawn thy liberty?

(I, 295)

When Abel refuses to give up his servile faith, Cain murders him to forestall the propagation of a race of slaves. As he explains later to his mother,

Am I my brother's keeper? Nay, by Heaven!
I am the keeper of the gates of life;
I guard the treasure of all humanity:
Mine, mine is life's inevitable trust,
Mine is the sacred heritage of man!
. . . .
How shall I suffer that such a traitor live
When by his life the future world is doomed
To stumble in the shadow of ignorance
Stung by the lash of self-inflicted fears?
Shall I not rather with violence even and death
Safeguard the treasure in jeopardy and keep
Flawless the sacred seed?

(I, 317)

Cain's violent action, which is the logical insanity of the Conservative Christian Anarchist, horrifies Eve; but, ultimately, she recognizes her son's deed as redemptive. Torn between love for him and the knowledge that he must live in exile, Eve courageously forsakes her maternal attachment and sends Cain upon his mission.

Cursed by Adam and by God, Cain embraces his fate, confident that his mother at least has understood. He prophesies a race of men who will follow his path of rebellion. They are, of course, to be Lodge's Conservative Christian Anarchists:

O I shall weary with all the woes of the world!
And when I shall lift up the immortal light
Like dawn in the dark places of men's souls,
And men shall hail it as a ruinous fire
Born for their world's destruction; they shall rise,
Nerved with ferocious fear, and hale me forth,
Seize me, traduce me, judge me, and condemn,—
And press the hemlock to my unshrinking lips
Or nail my scourged flesh naked to the cross!

(I, 338)

Since Eve will give birth to Seth, the murder of Abel has failed to
prevent the proliferation of degraded men. Cain foresees that violent confrontation between the spiritual descendants of Abel and
Cain is destined to recur in every generation, always to the same
result: the persecution of Sons of Man by slaves of orthodoxy.

II *Mythic Verse-Drama*

To Lodge's disappointment, the critical response to *Cain* was
mixed. Henry Adams praised it sardonically: "Although I am not
aware of ever having expressed an opinion which was not mistaken,
I will go so far, for once, as to say that Cain should put you high
among the poets of this century as far as we've gone [1904]. You
know best what this compliment is worth."[3] In the *Dial*, William
Morton Payne approved it heartily: "The diction of the poem is
almost as severe as its outline, and is sustained throughout at a lofty
pitch."[4] The *Nation* objected to the imperfect structure and to the
wordy first act, but the reviewer concluded that, "when all due
abatement has been made, 'Cain' is a book of interesting promise
. . . and there is here, moreover, in both substance and form,
much to reward attention."[5]

The reviewer in the *Independent* admired Lodge's energy but
dismissed his philosophy as immature: "Mr. Lodge's *Cain* is a verit-
able volcano of poetry, pouring out real fire mingled with smoke and
ashes. What Mr. Lodge lacks is the saving sense of humor. He has
undoubted force and passion . . . but the attempt to make a hero out
of Cain seems somehow very *young*."[6] In the most hostile review,
the critic in the *Harvard Graduates Magazine* compared *Cain* un-
favorably to Lord Byron's version: "Mr. Lodge is not a poet. For

him verse is apparently a matter of phrase, not of feeling. His language is full of strange turns and modern verbiage, which keep a reader marveling at his ingenuity and guessing at his meaning. . . . In the absence of redeeming qualities, his *Cain* cannot bear comparison with its predecessor, which it surpasses only in audacity."[7]

Although Lodge had been preceded in his use of the Cain legend by Byron and by Leconte de Lisle, Lodge's work was more closely related to a revival of mythic verse-drama at the turn of the century in America. Maurice F. Brown has argued that Lodge's *Cain* and *Herakles* form a coherent group with Santayana's *Lucifer*, Stickney's *Prometheus Pyrphoros*, and Moody's trilogy *The Masque of Judgment, The Fire Bringer*, and the unfinished *Death of Eve*. These Harvard poets, according to Brown, used mythic poetry to synthesize, through a complex dramatic form, the conflict they all perceived between humanistic and materialistic values. There was a strong tendency in these poets to "view myth as a repository of philosophical insight," but they carefully distinguished between myth and dogma. "Myth, for them, represented the imaginative expression of a universal human experience, while dogma was the temporary rational and moral framework imposed upon that experience."[8]

For Lodge, transcendental experience was always essentially irrational (even mystical) and amoral; and he regarded any attempt to rationalize or codify it, as in church theology, as a perversion of the "Truth." If dogma was dead or dying, myth embodied the immortality of archetype. Although the story of Cain as a basis for dogma lost its force as the church lost power to impose dogma, the myth of Cain as an archetype of the conflict between Conservative Christian Anarchism and orthodoxy retained its meaning.

Brown attributes the rise of mythic verse-drama to three factors: the general revival of interest in poetic drama, sponsored and encouraged by the leading American literary magazines in the 1890s; the explosion of knowledge in the field of comparative mythology, which was reflected in courses and lectures at Harvard in the 1890s; the failure of the Harvard Poets to find a lyric form large enough to encompass a vision based on a complex conflict of values. Of course, most of the major Romantic and Victorian poets had experimented with mythic verse-drama, and the Harvard group was not so much reviving as continuing a tradition.

The mythic verse-dramas of the Harvard Poets should be distinguished from the neoromantic plays of Percy MacKaye, Josephine Preston Peabody, and Ridgely Torrence, whose work, as Brown observes, "tended towards delicate fantasy or ponderous spectacle and pageantry." Whereas the Harvard Poets used myth to confront the complexities of contemporary thought, the dramatists used myth as a means of psychic regression. "Their plays most often represent an escape from materialism into an ideal world, a world of dream, portrayed either with lyric sweetness or heroic force. The dramatic action takes place in this ideal world and relies for its effect on a basic separation of the real and ideal."[9]

This kind of verse-drama resembled the Graustarkian mode in fiction and the nostalgic cult of childhood innocence in some of the boy books and autobiographies of the period—what Jay Martin has called the "daydream" of American regional writing. Martin has also detected a counterimpulse—the "nightmare of regionalism"—that "superimposes the present upon the past and proves, by insisting that only a defective past could have produced a present so incomplete and unsatisfying, that the daydream is mythical. . . . The daydream sings of the idyllic past-in-the-present; the nightmare, of the heritage of depravity. The daydreamer insists that the golden age lies just behind the veil of reality and might break through at any moment. The writers of nightmare find the past irretrievable and the present irredeemable."[10]

The Harvard Poets, like the best regional writers, manifested tendencies toward both the "daydream" and the "nightmare." But, whereas the regional writers tended to express their double vision ironically, the Harvard group tended to superimpose the mythic past upon the present—not to emphasize the gulf between them but to suggest that, if the past is irretrievable, the present might still be redeemed by assimilation and reinterpretation of Classical and Biblical myths. In their affirmation of myth as a possible bridge between the past and the present, Lodge and his Harvard contemporaries anticipated the work of Modernist poets like Pound and Eliot who, less confident of synthesizing humanistic and materialistic values, would adopt an ironic rather than prophetic tone.

Thomas Riggs has said of Lodge's verse-dramas that, "like Prometheus's vultures, they return over and over again to the theme of rebirth: the great need for it, the overpowering sense of guilt that accompanies the assassination of the shapes that tie the poet to his paternity."[11] The dissolution of family ties became a central theme in all of Lodge's work after 1901: from the broken marriages in his novels to the tragic division of family loyalties in *Cain* and in the unpublished opera "The Castle of Fear" to the murder by Herakles of his children. To some contemporary readers, *Cain* seemed patently autobiographical. Margaret Terry Chanler recalled that, "without Bay's intention, it was easy to recognize Senator Lodge in the rather crusty progenitor of the human race, while the part of Eve could only fall to the beautiful and infinitely tactful lady, his wife. Cain was of course the spokesman for Bay's own feelings."[12] "I was really interested in Bay's Cain," Henry Adams wrote to Stoddard, "and thought the Senator feeble as Adam and Mrs. Lodge *trés réussie* as Eve."[13] There is considerable evidence in Lodge's poems and letters to support an interpretation of *Cain* as an expression of Lodge's Oedipal conflicts.

In light of Lodge's philosophy, it is clear that a Conservative Christian Anarchist would inevitably come into conflict with his parents and even with his own wife and children. After all, Lodge's line of poet-seers included no men burdened with family. It may be that through the actions of his poet-heroes, Lodge carried out imaginatively an assassination of paternity and its responsibilities. No doubt Lodge feared, at least preconsciously, that his life roles as husband, father, and son threatened his idealistic aspirations. As he wrote to his mother in 1898,

My mind is like a constant nightmare to me—I think the pain of life must increase in direct proportion to the strength of the Spiritual desires & aspirations in a man: for as his Spiritual hope grows to certainty the constant tearing of the human earthly longings in him must grow more acute & more agonizing. I think it is only on this theory one can perceive the awful martyrdom of a life like Christ's or St. Francis' or Buddha's. And for the rest of us with our scant visions & weak faiths we suffer in proportion as we desire & love the little we have seen & the much we have wanted to believe of the region of Spiritual things. We suffer because we are constantly thrust back by the irresistable force of our own lives[,] constantly blinded & choked & must begin laboriously again our poor edifice of beauty & light.[14]

That the Schopenhauerian ideas of this letter ever caused Lodge to slight his domestic responsibilities is problematical, for no evidence exists of obvious discord between Lodge and his wife or between Lodge and his parents. On the contrary, Lodge seems to have had a remarkably happy marriage, to have been a devoted father, and to have had close relationships with his parents. Yet the preoccupation of Lodge's later work with violent dissolution of familial ties suggests that deep-seated insecurity and hostility may have festered beneath the calm surface of his domestic life.

Although Lodge may have participated vicariously in the defiant Conservative Christian Anarchism of his heroes, he understood that literal application of his philosophy to everyday life was impossible. He chose to live torn between his spiritual ideals and his mundane responsibilities. As his poetry came to emphasize, he anticipated relief from this tension only in death.

III The Great Adventure

In reviewing *Poems*, the *Nation* complained, "We regret to find that this author, although thirty years old and eight years out of college, still lingers in the sophomoric period. . . . It is to be feared that we must look to some high purpose or deep and genuine grief to bring him to maturity."[15] Deep and genuine grief came to George Cabot Lodge in October, 1904, with the sudden death of Trumbull Stickney. His death not only precipitated the severest emotional crisis of Lodge's life but affected his poetry after 1904 by giving it the imprint of anguish. During his eight years in Paris between 1895 and 1903, Trumbull Stickney had patiently earned the academic credentials Lodge had been too impatient to pursue. Stickney became the first American awarded the *Doctorat ès Lettres* by the Sorbonne, and he accepted a position as an instructor of Greek at Harvard. He completed the first semester in apparent good health; but during 1904 he began to suffer severe headaches, which persisted through the spring term. By June, his vision had partially failed, and Stickney finally agreed in August to a physical examination. The diagnosis was a brain tumor.

When Lodge learned of Stickney's condition, he was stunned. "I am completely unnerved," he wrote to his wife. "I feel at present utterly prostrated. Somehow I have never conceived of Joe's dying."[16] Lodge fled to Tuckernuck, where he had planned a vacation with Stickney. Clinging to a faint hope of his friend's recovery, Lodge relived in his mind "all the immense days and ways of life that we have seen together."[17] As always, Tuckernuck calmed his nerves; and Lodge returned to Boston in September to help care for Stickney, who was now blind and in his final days. For Lodge, Stickney's loss was psychologically devastating; and the writing of a sonnet cycle to his memory became therapeutic. As Lodge explained to his mother in the summer of 1905, "I believe there are

but two ways with real grief: get rid of it if you can; but if you can't,
then take all you can get of it, live in it, work in it, experience it as
far as you are capable of experiencing anything. Let it nourish you!
as it will, as anything will that is real, and in direct proportion to its
reality and significance."[18]

Unable to rid himself of grief, Lodge immersed himself imaginatively in it. The resulting poems in *The Great Adventure* sounded a
new note for him—one different from both the youthful pessimism
of *The Song of the Wave* and the strenuous affirmation of *Cain*.
Lodge reasserted a faith in the reality of transcendental experience
but a faith tempered by a profound awareness of mortality. As
Henry Adams noted, Lodge's *Great Adventure* "probably marked
the instant when life did, in fact, hover between the two motives,—
the beginning and the end,—Love and Death. Both were, for the
moment, in full view, equally near, and equally intense, with the
same background of the unknown."[19]

Lodge divided *The Great Adventure* into three sections of twenty-
six sonnets each: "Life" (dedicated to Bigelow); "Love" (dedicated to
his wife); "Death" (dedicated to Stickney). Only in "Death," which
is a roughly chronological account of Stickney's death and its aftermath, did Lodge attempt to create a sonnet cycle. Each of the
sections moves from faith to doubt to muted reaffirmation, but there
is no strict development from poem to poem. The central theme of
the volume is the spiritual quest, once described by Stickney as
"The Great Adventure":

> He said: "We are the Great Adventurers,
>   This is the Great Adventure: thus to be
>   Alive and, on the universal sea
>   Of being, lone yet dauntless mariners.
> In the rapt outlook of astronomers
>   To rise thro' constellated gyres of thought;
>   To fall with shattered pinions, overwrought
>   With flight, like unrecorded Lucifers:—
> Thus to receive identity, and thus
>   Return at last to the dark element,—
>   This is the Great Adventure!" All of us,
> Who saw his dead, deep-visioned eyes, could see,
>   After the Great Adventure, immanent,
>   Splendid and strange, the Great Discovery!
>   (II, 70)

In the closing lines of this poem, as in several sonnets in the "Death" section, Lodge affirmed that some "Great Discovery" lies behind the veil of death. At the instant of Stickney's death, just as Lodge had imagined of Jesus on the cross, a deeper revelation seemed to flash in his sightless eyes:

> His eyes seemed darkly to discern a goal,—
> And we beheld the daybreak's boundless breath
> Glimmer against the windows of his soul.
>
> (II, 63)

> And we, who kept the vigil by his side,
> Saw, when at last the door was opened wide,
> Flash in his eyes the Dawn his soul pursued.
>
> (II, 65)

> Until at last, after prodigious days,
> Outcast over the precipice of Time,
> His eyes, triumphant, cried: "The Light! The Light!"
>
> (II, 66)

Lodge explained the spiritual meaning of Stickney's vision in the concluding poem of the volume:

> It is not that we loved him, as in sooth
> Beyond all words we loved and love him still;
> It is not that he seemed so to fulfil
> Ineffably the very spirit of Truth;
> It is not, day by day, in the uncouth
> Brutality of death, his calm control,
> Courage and tenderness of heart and soul;
> It is not pity even of his mere youth;—
> God knows these were alone sufficient cause!
> Yet it is not for all these things that we
> Now keep sure faith with things transcendent, true
> And untransmissible:—it is because,
> Even in the presence of the Mystery,
> He knew!—it is because we knew he knew!
>
> (II, 86)

If the "Mystery" becomes transfigured for the dead, it remains a "baffling silence" (II, 17) for the living. A "faith with things tran-

scendent" is constantly shaken by ghoulish questions, the answers to
which continuously recede:

> Questions
> Curious of life and love and death they stand
>   Outward along the shadowy verge of thought;
>   Rebels and deicides, they rise unsought
> And spare no creed and yield to no command.
> Even tho' at last we seem to understand,
>   Yet, when our eyes grow sphered to the new light,
>   We find them, outposts in the forward night,
> Their eyes still restless with the same demand.
> On all the heights and at the farthest goal
>   Set by the seers and christs of yesterday
>   They watch and wait and ask the onward way;
> They storm the citadels of faith and youth,
>   And, gazing always for the stars of Truth,
> Crowd in the glimmering windows of the Soul.
>
> (II, 27)

The stars, which throughout the volume symbolize "Truth," seem
too remote to reach in life. The quest becomes a lonely and endless
journey, fraught with pain and doubt.

Throughout *The Great Adventure*, faith and doubt rage in tension. The affirmation of one poem is qualified by the uncertainty of
another; Lodge in some sonnets seems to be willing himself to
believe. One may consider, for example, his revision of "To Night,"
which, as published in the *Century*, had expressed in its sestet a
tentative faith:

> Thus may we feel how changing avatars
>   Shall so complete us that, perchance, when we
>   Transcend the throes of spiritual strife
> And learn the deep tranquillity of stars,
>   The ineffable presence of Eternity
>   Shall find a mansion in the House of Life.[20]

In *The Great Adventure*, Lodge changed the conditional language to
make the sestet unequivocal:

> Thou shalt complete us all who love and learn
>   The secret of thy silences, till we
>   Arise regenerate from the throes of strife,

> And in thine all-receptive peace discern
> The ineffable presence of eternity
> Waiting forever at the gates of life.
> (II, 28)

The two versions of "To Night" epitomize Lodge's wavering between faith and doubt in the volume. The transcendental vision is glimpsed through nature, friendship, or sexual love only to be eclipsed again by the mortal reality of time. Even the "Love" section, which celebrates the sacramental power of sexual love, collapses occasionally into uncertainity. In the moment of sexual union, which Lodge associates with religious ecstasy, time stands still:

> That day of the innumerable days
> Was like a gate set open secretly,
> Where the swift sense of immortality
> Drave us from Time's interminable ways.
> . . . .
> We saw how blind and aimless on and on
> Time journeys, while the ripened harvests stand
> Of Truth and Liberty on either hand;
> And so we reaped and made the sacred bread
> And poured the wine of Love's communion:
> And there that day the starving soul was fed.
> (II, 41)

Through love, the transcendental vision is revealed:

> We felt the birth of poems, the springs of song;
> And saw, by winds of music borne along,
> Our souls go forth on love's high seas, like ships
> Making Truth's voyage without helm or chart.
> (II, 43)

In retrospect, however, the vision recedes to dream, perhaps to nightmare, and hurls the dreamer back upon mortality:

> She stood in the weird moonlight of a dream,
> And in the light there was incredible
> Silence, and on her lips no syllable
> Of any speech, and in her eyes no gleam.
> . . . .

And terribly I felt there was no stir
    But only silence in the heart of her,
    And silence in her soul!—Then was I hurled
Back into life, and woke, and knew that she,
    In moonlit silence, somewhere in the world
    Waited alone and motionless for me.
                                        (II, 47)

The glory of vision can survive in memory, man's only way of
stopping or reversing time; but memory itself will be annihilated in
time:

In Time's cathedral Memory, like a ghost
    Crouched in the narrow twilight of the nave,
    Fumbles with thin pathetic hands to save
Relics of all things lived and loved and lost.
Life fares and feasts and Memory counts the cost
    With unrelenting lips that dare confess
    Life's secret failures, sins and loneliness
And life's exalted hopes, defiled and crossed.
Shalt thou endure, O Memory, and thy breath
    Quicken the dead in thy dominion
    And fire the peaks of thought we dared to climb,
When, in the swift relentless chill of death,
    The crawling ice-floes of oblivion
    Strangle thy passage thro' the seas of Time?
                                        (II, 24)

Days that have been and nevermore shall be,
    Children of Time the sword of Time has slain,
    Great hours of life when heart and soul were fain
Of Love's pure fire and Truth's eternity,—
Now, on the marches of that dim domain
    And desolate sunset-land of Memory,
    Ye rise like tortured ghosts and silently
Walk in the sombre twilights of the brain.
And we, like pilgrims on the path of Time
    Who find no rest nor any dwelling-place,
    We follow blindly in Life's retinue,
While, like the furies of Orestes' crime,
    The spectral hosts of Memory on our trace
    Innumerably assemble and pursue.
                                        (II, 26)

These sonnets, among the best Lodge ever wrote, expose the horror of doubt that underlies Lodge's cosmic optimism. After 1905, Lodge continued to proclaim man's need to seek the "soul's inheritance," but he did so with increasing awareness of the difficulties of the quest.

Most of the sonnets in *The Great Adventure* demonstrate poetic competence, and several achieve genuine power. Lodge did not hesitate to experiment with the form; he used slant rhymes, sight rhymes, and irregular lines, and he attempted several tetrameter sonnets. Although some reviewers took him to task for violating strict sonnet form, the critical response was generally enthusiastic. William Morton Payne in the *Dial* wrote that "high praise must be given to the thoughtful and imaginative qualities of Mr. Lodge's verse; he is a poet who is visibly growing with each new volume he puts forth, and who may be expected to go far."[21] Ferris Greenslet, in a review that dismissed E. A. Robinson as a "minor poet," credited Lodge with "a passionate rush to his thought."[22]

Louise Collier Willcox, in the prestigious *North American Review*, called *The Great Adventure* "the finest collection of sonnets since Rossetti's 'House of Life.' " She was disturbed, however, by Lodge's characteristic love of abstraction: "If one hesitates to say the word 'great' of them, the fault lies rather with the theme than with the execution. It is almost too abstract for form, and from time to time, in reading them as a connected whole, one has that sense of barrenness which results from the lack of all concrete images."[23] This last point was amplified by the review in the *Harvard Graduates Magazine*: "We cannot help wondering whether Mr. Lodge's surge of phrases corresponds to any actual thought, to any real emotion; it suggests too often the Swinburnian emptiness."[24] This judgment, fair enough if applied to the early volumes, failed to recognize the imaginative maturity of *The Great Adventure*. Perhaps for the first time, Lodge expressed a theme worthy of his "surge of phrases." In the best of *The Great Adventure*, Lodge came of age as a poet.

IV *Poems of Trumbull Stickney*

If Lodge triumphed over grief in writing *The Great Adventure*, his editing of Stickney's poems during the summer of 1905 revived his mental anguish. Before his death, Stickney had appointed Lodge, his brother John Ellerton Lodge, and William Vaughn

Moody to be his literary executors; and he had charged them to prepare a volume of his collected poems. Stickney and Moody had been close since their days on the *Harvard Monthly;* but although Lodge may have met Moody at Harvard, they had never been friends. What Stickney had hoped would be a harmonious working relationship soon degenerated into bickering and recriminations between Lodge and Moody.

The editorial project began smoothly. Lodge had read and edited all of Stickney's manuscripts by early February, 1905, and had turned them over to Moody at a meeting in New York. Moody at first agreed to delete all poems to which the editors could not give unanimous approval, but ultimately his more inclusive policy prevailed. "I feel that it is far more important to include everything of positive value, even though it may not appeal to all of us with equal force, than to make a collection to which no one will object. . . . I mean that we had better run the risk of including too much, rather than to exclude anything concerning which any one of us has a deep conviction of worth."[25] By March, the contents of the volume were established; and Lodge, who financed the book, was negotiating with Houghton Mifflin.

Unfortunately, a basic disagreement on editorial policy arose. Lodge wanted to annex interpretive and biographical footnotes to every poem. In this regard, he asked Moody to submit an acknowledgment of the debt of his *Fire Bringer* to Stickney's *Prometheus Pyrphoros*. Moody, who believed "it would be better to let the poems speak for themselves,"[26] felt it inappropriate and unnecessary to record his debt to Stickney in this volume; but, as a compromise, he agreed to write the acknowledgment if Lodge would unobtrusively incorporate it into the proposed biographical preface he would write. Under terrible strain, Lodge finished the preface on June 20; unsatisfied with it but too exhausted to continue, Lodge sent one copy to Moody, another to the Stickney family, and a third to Houghton Mifflin to be set in type.

The Stickney preface reflected Lodge's emotional stress. In twenty-eight tortured pages, Lodge tried to express the spiritual meaning of Stickney's life and death; he dwelt on an abstract description of the anarchist-poet, whom he felt Stickney had personified. Lodge's style, apparently an attempt at a poetic prose suitable to his lofty theme, was a pseudophilosophical muddle. One example will suffice: "For poetry, the musical composition of words, expresses, certainly, not a single faculty or several faculties in the presence of their several objects and functions, but rather,—speaking ideally, as we now profess to speak,—the whole man in presence of the whole universe."[27] Only in the final paragraphs in which he focused on personal memories of Stickney did Lodge achieve coherence. Lodge was capable of writing cogent prose, and the disaster of the Stickney preface was caused more by Lodge's unsettled frame of mind than by a failure of style.

Meanwhile, Moody, recovering in Chicago from an operation and engrossed in writing *The Great Divide*, was anxious to dispatch his responsibilities on the Stickney volume. He had expected from Lodge a short, factual biography, not a long, speculative tract. Unaware of Lodge's emotional investment in the preface, Moody recommended its deletion. He advised Lodge to publish the essay in the *Atlantic Monthly* or some other magazine where it would reach a larger audience and, he hoped, promote the Stickney volume. Lodge, hurt and angered, pleaded that, since the preface had been set in type and approved by the Stickney family, it should be printed. Moody, furious that Lodge had sent the preface to the publisher without his approval, proposed that the dispute be arbitrated by a disinterested outsider. He suggested also that Lodge substitute for his essay the three sonnets to Stickney that had recently appeared in *Scribner's*.

Lodge accused Moody of insincerity and strenuously objected to the intervention of an outsider on the grounds that Stickney had given exclusive authority over the volume to his executors. Moody repented: "The fact is, then that I could not approve your memoir as a whole, though I liked parts of it. . . . The fact is also that in counseling against printing any memoirs whatever I wished by indirection to dissuade you from printing yours. My words were therefore in some measure disingenuous, and for this I beg your pardon."[28] As a conciliatory gesture, Moody agreed again to supply in galley proofs a footnote of his indebtedness to *Prometheus Pyrphoros* and to accept John Lodge's decision as to the fate of the preface. Wisely, John Lodge voted to condense it to a factual sketch.

But just when their differences appeared resolved, the quarrel exploded. In galley proofs Lodge added a lengthy interpretive footnote on "Julian" in which he editorialized against the orthodox church. Moody, who lost his patience, angrily demanded the excision of all editorial apparatus, including his acknowledgment; he threatened to resign as editor if his conditions were not met. Lodge, in outrage, accused Moody of intellectual dishonesty and Moody retorted, "I must repudiate with the strongest emphasis the imputation, conveyed in your letter just received, that in objecting to the insertion of the Prometheus note I have had any intention or desire to refrain from making the acknowledgment due Stickney."[29] Although Moody bitterly resented Lodge's allegations, he conceded that, in return for dropping the preface, Lodge had the right to demand the acknowledgment. This he reluctantly supplied. Lodge trimmed the preface to a skeleton of facts and deleted the footnote. A volume that satisfied none of the editors finally went to press in September.

It is fair to say that throughout the quarrel Moody was more sinned against than sinning. Although Lodge complained to his mother that Moody was delaying the completion of the volume, Moody seemingly worked as quickly as possible under the circumstances of his illness and his other literary activities. His editorial policy was probably the correct one for a volume meant to introduce a hitherto neglected poet, for Stickney would be recognized only because of the merits of his verse; and Lodge's preface and interpretive notes would have obfuscated his friend's poetry. Certainly, Lodge's belligerence over the acknowledgment placed Moody in an unfair position. In fact, throughout the affair Lodge seemed to use disagreement over editorial policy as a pretext for a deeper hostility that was founded perhaps on personal and professional jealousy. Lodge had always considered Stickney his best friend; and he may have resented collaborating (on what he considered a labor of love) with a relative stranger who had not shared Stickney's tortured final hours. Moreover, Lodge may have envied Moody's success as a writer. Moody's reputation was at its height in 1905, and in the midst of the project, he was elected to the National Institute of Arts and Letters, an honor Lodge would not receive for three years.

In the final analysis, however, Lodge's overwrought behavior should be attributed more to the appalling stress under which he worked than to any malice. To his credit, he took the conciliatory initiative by writing Moody in 1906 to compliment him on his article on Stickney in the *North American Review*. Moody replied in kind: "Someday I want to write you a letter to tell you how high and strong a pleasure your sonnet sequence about Joe gave and yet gives me."[30] Such a letter is not extant, and it is unlikely that Moody and Lodge had any further association.

CHAPTER 5

Herakles

THE publication of *The Great Adventure* seemed to signal a hopeful turn in Lodge's literary fortunes. Perhaps as a result of favorable reviews, the volume sold over four hundred copies, hardly the record of a best-seller, but nearly twice as many copies as *Cain* had sold. "I imagine that there are about five hundred Americans who read poetry, and you must have reached nearly all," Adams told him. "It is no small success. Indeed I believe you have no rival."[1] Adams's cynical estimate of the size of the American audience for poetry helps to explain certain paradoxical events of Lodge's last years.

If the decade 1900–1910 witnessed a revolution in the language of American poetry, it also marked the emergence of a revised theory about the audience for American poetry. Belief in the existence of an educated, or at least literate, "middlebrow" audience, which had sustained the Fireside Poets, yielded to a Tory dialectical view of American culture. The "middlebrow" audience, which may have been a myth, appeared to split into "highbrow" and "lowbrow" components. These terms were invented by Van Wyck Brooks in 1915 for a cultural thesis that had been gradually developing in Harvard circles since the Civil War and that was widely held in Lodge's literary generation. It does not matter so much whether or not Brooks (or Adams or Santayana from whom Brooks borrowed the idea) was correct, but it is significant that Lodge acted as if he were. The "highbrow-lowbrow" dialectic sprang from the same *fin de siècle* pessimism that informed Lodge's Conservative Christian Anarchism, and it has persisted to the present as an orthodoxy of literary history. Lodge became one of many writers torn between its terms.

From Harvard days forward, Lodge had dreamed of commanding the attention and the adulation of a society whose moral bases his

poetry was meant to subvert. Contrary to the central assumptions of
Conservative Christian Anarchism, Lodge hoped somehow to fuse
the roles of anarchist and Brahmin sage, at once to knit his ideas into
the fabric of society and to retain the perspective of alienation. After
1906, Lodge increasingly agreed with Adams that his work could
never win popular acceptance and that, if any audience existed for
his poetry, it must by necessity comprise an elite saving remnant.

I The Megaphone of Oratory

During the summer of 1905, Lodge, inspired by rereading
Stickney's *Prometheus Pyrphoros*, decided to write his own version
of the Prometheus myth. From its inception, Lodge regarded the
writing of *Herakles* as his most ambitious work. "It will be a long
job," he told Mitchell; "God knows (you'll excuse the archaic but
picturesque phrase) whether or not I shall come out ahead on it."[2]
Embroiled throughout the winter of 1905–06 in the construction of
his Washington house, - Lodge could not concentrate on *Herakles*.
Lodge always required long periods of isolation in order to write;
and the more he felt himself "thoroughly dissipated in the meticul-
ous attention to material trifles," the more he felt urged to withdraw
into himself. "I feel terribly hampered & thwarted by the many
little things of daily & social life," he told Mitchell. "The anchorites
& the Solitaries had in them much wisdom & the time is near when
I shall crudely sacrifice everything including my family to preserve
that retirement, that spaciousness & even flow of Time which must
be had if the voice of God within me is to be heard."[3]

To cheer his friend, Mitchell suggested that Lodge put *Herakles*
aside and try his hand at a stage play. Lodge and Mitchell had
discussed the state of the American theater two years before. "It's
depressing beyond measure," Lodge had said, "to know that the
American theatre is reserved exclusively, either for importations, or
the worthless manufactures of almost illiterate Americans who regard plays merely as merchandise, and who would manufacture
boots with equal enjoyment and success."[4] Like the serious poet,
the serious playwright seemed to have no audience, or a small one at
best. After 1906, Lodge felt at times that he wrote only for himself,
but he saw an advantage in the situation:

I should have but one personal advantage in writing a play, namely a
genuine indifference as to its being played or being successful if played. I
call this an advantage because it eliminates the possibility of my mind being

disturbed and my powers consequently impaired by any influences external to myself. I become increasingly convinced that precisely as perfection of being consists in a perfectly transparent reality, so artistic perfection depends upon the degree to which the artist speaks his own words in his own voice and is unhampered by the vocabulary of convention and the megaphone of oratory—which exists and could exist only on the theory of an omnipresent multitude . . . . The whole core of the struggle, for ourselves and for art, is to emerge from the envelope of thoughts and words and deeds which are not our own, but the laws and conventions and traditions formed of a kind of composite of other men's ideas and emotions and prejudices.[5]

Unfortunately, Lodge never fully achieved in his art the ideal expressed in this letter. His worst poetry stood at one extreme as a "composite of other men's ideas and emotions and prejudices" and, at the other, as so perfect a "transparent reality" that it was visible only to Lodge himself. Of course, a poet who could utter unique thoughts in a totally unconventional language probably has never existed. If he had, he would have had no readers, for no one could have understood him. Lodge, feeling that he had no readers, seemed to believe the converse of this proposition: that, if a poet has no audience, it is because the purity of his language and the perfection of his thoughts exceed the comprehension of an audience whose mental powers have been stunted by life in a commercial culture.

Ironically, at a moment when Lodge most felt the need for isolation, he was offered a chance to take up the "vocabulary of convention and the megaphone of oratory." Self-consciously, he told Mitchell:

I've been asked (peals of Homeric and scornful laughter from Mitchell) to deliver the poem at the Phi Beta Kappa in Cambridge this spring—June. (Mitchell chokes with mirth and shows symptoms of strangulation. Is patted on the back and recovers. Lodge then good-naturedly continues:) You observe how low I've sunk and for a punishment for your superior sneers I'm going to send you my poem for the occasion to read and criticize. (Mitchell sourly admits that the joke is not entirely on Lodge.) I shall send it soon, in fact it may arrive any day.[6]

Theoretically, a poet-anarchist should not receive, certainly not accept, such invitations; and a touch of embarrassment existed beneath Lodge's humor.

He anticipated his first confrontation with a live audience with apprehension as well as excitement. Lodge poured his energies into

the writing of "The Soul's Inheritance," a blank-verse poem of a
hundred and fifty-three lines, which sounded the familiar refrain of
transcendence:

> Magnificent presence of the living Truth—
> We know not when thy swift, serene, strong flame
> Shall violate our sanctuaries of sleep!
> We know not when, from carnal lethargies
> And trivial pastimes and derisive dreams
> Of ineffectual felicities,
> Irresolutions and timidities
> And temperate ambitions, we shall wake
> To find our safe exclusions overborne,
> The pale of our defence invaded, all
> Our precincts of secure retreat destroyed;
> To feel the dark enchantments yield; to hear
> Thy trumpets blowing in our citadels.
> . . . .
> Thou shalt appear, imperishable Truth,
> Spirit of Liberty!—but well we know
> That life and death are only thine adventure.
> And well we know the time of revelation
> Is always now—eternity is now!
> The place of miracles is always here—
> Infinity is here! Then here and now,
> And in thy name, O latent Truth within us,
> In thought and word and deed, in life and death,
> Let us report and celebrate the soul!
>
> (II, 89–90)

The audience, which included many friends and relatives, reacted
with thunderous approval. One listener later reported that "Dr.
Huntington, who was at Harvard told Lucy [Frelinghuysen] that
Bay's poem was the most wonderful thing that he had ever heard,
that the ovation he received was overwhelming. That instead of
reading from a manuscript he had memorized the whole thing, and
without a pause had recited it—for fifty-minutes. That his language,
his thoughts, his theme, were all in the most elevated and cultivated
style . . . . I am glad that we can be proud of him, even if we do not
understand him."[7] As Lodge intoned his verse to Harvard's intellectual elite, he must have felt that his thoughts would at last reach an
audience capable of understanding them. Many in the crowd, however, like Dr. Huntington, were probably more impressed by

Lodge's solemn manner and by the "elevated and cultivated style"
of "The Soul's Inheritance" than by its philosophical import. To a
listener unfamiliar with Lodge's other work, his words may have
seemed more a rhetoric suited to the pomp of the occasion than a
serious philosophy. Even a sympathetic listener like Edith Wharton
found the poem disappointing. "I agree with all you say about Bay's
poem," she admitted to Sara Norton; "alas but it is not Europe, or
opportunity of any kind, he lacks; it is the real intrinsic higher sense
of beauty—visible beauty especially. He doesn't see things in images. Still—it was well done."[8]

After his appearance in Cambridge, Lodge received an invitation
to deliver a poem about the Pilgrims before the annual meeting in
December of the New England Society of New York. Lodge saw an
analogy between the perilous journey of the Pilgrims and the gruel-
ing pilgrimage of the soul toward perfection, and he warned the
chairman of the dinner that his poem "would take the Pilgrims
rather for its text than its subject."[9] Besides Lodge's "Pilgrims," the
program included speeches about education by the presidents of the
University of Virginia and Trinity College and an account by Robert
E. Peary of his Arctic explorations. For an audience composed
largely of New York businessmen, Peary's talk was probably the
featured attraction; and many listeners must have been puzzled by
Lodge's ambitious and lofty lines:

> May we with haughtier strength and hardihood
> Send forth the vagrant and victorious soul
> From dreams and desolate insanities
> And gross deceptions of the solid world,
> Into the shining night, on to the Road!
> Well may we know it lies before us still,
> Who are the Pilgrims, as it stretched for them
> Whose pilgrimage is done!—the self-same road,
> Hazardous, hard, unknown, which leads afar,
> Thro' lusts and lies, thro' laws and governments,
> Thro' settled customs and established creeds,—
> Thro' all substantial things and sensible forms.
> And well for us if we may find it out
> And walk thereon our spiritual way
> Forward to real achievements and progressions,—
> Pilgrims, as once they were, in high resolve
> Launched on the Pilgrimage that once was theirs!
>   (II, 100–01)

As Adams said, "The theme, on such an occasion and before such an audience, in the fumes of dinner and tobacco, was adventurous."[10]

Lodge may have detected indifference behind his audience's polite applause, for, after the New England Society dinner, he did not attempt to bridge again the gap he sensed between himself and the popular audience or even the cultivated audience. As he consciously withdrew from the public arena during 1907, Lodge felt the gap widening into an abyss. In this regard, Henry Adams was right:

However much he tried, and the more he tried, to lessen the gap between himself—his group of personal friends—and the public, the gap grew steadily wider; the circle of sympathies enlarged itself not at all, or with desperate slowness; and this consciousness of losing ground,—of failure to find a larger horizon of friendship beyond his intimacy;—the growing fear that, beyond this narrow range, no friends existed in the immense void of society,—or could exist, in the form of society which he lived in,—the suffocating sense of talking and singing in a vacuum that allowed no echo to return, grew more and more oppressive with each effort to overcome it.[11]

II   The End Looms Large

The direction of Lodge's life and work took a drastic, irreversible turn during 1907. Forsaking hope of popular success, Lodge cut his ties to the mass audience by submitting no poetry to the magazines until shortly before his death. He began to regard *Herakles* as his *magnum opus*—an accomplishment only a select handful of his friends would ever see. In a revealing letter to Marjorie Nott, a friend since childhood, Lodge expressed his almost desperate sense of failure:

I am . . . drawing to the close of the immense piece of work which has held and compelled me for a year past. The end looms large in my prospect and I am doing my best,—as you shall one day see. You, in fact, will be one of only a half-dozen, at best, who will see it. Which is, I imagine, all to my credit; and certainly as much as I reasonably want. What I have learned in the last year, through the work and the days, I shall never live to express; which is, I take it, illustrative . . . of the radical inferiority of writing your truth instead of being and living it,—namely that by writing you can never, at all, keep abreast of it, but inevitably fall more and more behind as your pace betters. So I shall eventually perish having consciously failed, with . . . "all my epigrams in me." I wonder if Jesus consciously failed. . . . I mean, did he have that consciousness of personal, solitary failure, which one can hardly . . . dissociate from the religious being of the soul of man?[12]

Besides Lodge's acute sense of isolation, one important cause of his increasing darkness of mind after 1907 was his failing health. When he told Marjorie Nott that "the end looms large," Lodge may have been referring to more than the expected completion of *Herakles;* for Lodge learned in the fall of 1907 that his life might be coming to an end. "I've had a beastly autumn in many ways," he told Mitchell. "I was knocked out by Malaria—in the process of which my rather second-rate heart went singularly queer, a fact which I've told no one but you—that is just how singularly queer it went—for I don't want my mother or Bessy to be worried more than is necessary . . . . I've been a little fussed about my heart taken in connection with the fact that my 'Heracles'—which signifies such endless things to me—is only just three quarters done."[13] There was probably no direct medical connection between Lodge's malaria and a sudden weakening of his heart; his condition more likely resulted from an undiagnosed case of rheumatic fever.[14] In any event, Lodge knew that he had to conserve his strength if he were to finish *Herakles.* Consequently, he sacrificed all social life, including a visit to Mitchell in New York, during the winter of 1907–08. He even declined to attend the annual dinner of the National Institute of Arts and Letters, to which he had been elected on February 20, 1908.

Late in the spring of 1908, Lodge concluded nearly three years of work on *Herakles.* He sent the manuscript to Mitchell, who, aware of the importance of *Herakles* to Lodge, provided the praise and encouragement his friend so desperately needed. Lodge could hardly express his gratitude and joy. Hopeful that a vacation would restore his health, Lodge planned a trip to Europe with his parents for the summer of 1908. Before sailing in July, he contracted with Houghton Mifflin for November publication of *Herakles.* In his letters to his wife from Europe, Lodge's sense of mortality cast a darker light on formerly bright surroundings. These letters sound like the haunted ruminations of an old man; and, in fact, during his last year of life, Lodge seemed to age well beyond his thirty-five years. The brooding voice of the Noctambulist gradually came to drown out the cry of youth, energy, and faith that he had voiced once more in *Herakles.*

III *A Half-hewn Masterpiece*

Although Henry Adams admired the ambitiousness of *Herakles,* the Promethean scale of the drama bewildered him. "It was an immense effort," Adams wrote; "and in approaching the analysis of this drama, which, in bulk, is nearly equal to all the rest of the poet's writings together, and in sustained stress stands beyond comparison with them, the critic or biographer is embarrassed, like the poet himself, by the very magnitude of the scheme.[15] The poetic task Lodge set himself in *Herakles* was awesome; for he proposed to poeticize a myth that, as Adams accurately indicated, had never been handled with complete success. Furthermore, Lodge chose a form, the blank-verse drama, in which few if any poets had ever succeeded. Lodge viewed his life and work as an effort to scale the "impossible height"; that *Herakles* should fail seemed almost predetermined in Lodge's mind. Yet, if *Herakles* is at best a half-hewn masterpiece, it contains passages and scenes of immense dramatic power. Like Michelangelo's unfinished *Saint Matthew* which is imprisoned in a half-carved block of stone, Lodge's figure of Herakles seems straining to emerge in his full dimensions.

E. A. Robinson, who called *Herakles* "undoubtedly one of the most significant poems of modern times,"[16] was probably impressed more by Lodge's theme than by his verse; for like Robinson, Lodge was seeking light in a world perpetually in shadows. Based on the Hercules legend, as told by Diodorus Siculus, *Herakles* depicts the hero's awakening into transcendental glory. Through most of the twelve scenes of the drama, Herakles is in search of spiritual fulfillment but is uncertain of the path to follow. He is surrounded by characters who represent attitudes that would divert him from his quest; and his strongest antagonists are Creon, who represents worldly power and skepticism, and Megara, who represents domesticity and resignation. These and other attitudes Herakles must reject if he is to discover his self-divinity; but only gradually, in scenes eight through ten, does he learn the horrible price of transcendence: the violent severance of every bond to the human community. Like Cain, Herakles must murder to create the new self; and when Herakles slaughters his children in scene ten, his action is as "redemptive" as Cain's killing of Abel. In the concluding two scenes, Herakles, now a full-fledged Conservative Christian Anarchist, justifies himself to his family, and undertakes the first of his heroic labors—the freeing of Prometheus.

The drama opens with a dialogue between the Woman and the Poet, who serve throughout as a chorus. Both are seeking the light of spiritual experience. The Woman, who represents carnal love,

tempts the Poet to abandon the quest; but the Poet insists that he
has forsaken physical passion:

> I have learned
> How, in the last fulfilment of the spirit,
> There is a nobler end for life than love,
> There is a nobler end for love than you!
>
> (II, 191)

The Woman ridicules him, claiming that poetry itself is an expression of man's animality:

> O you are wise—in words! You are a poet!
> The cheat is not too plain. Yet one discerns
> How you are chafed and sharpened with desire!
> The thrill strikes thro'—and you make poems of it,
> Since there's imagination left at least
> To prove us how we are not respectable
> And give to lust a lyric rapture:—Yes!
> Tamed tho' he be, the animal will sing!
>
> (II, 193)

The Poet reiterates his faith in "a nobler end" and swears to search
for light "whether the quest prove real or vain," Converted by the
Poet's conviction, the Woman agrees to join him in the quest.

Herakles too is seeking light. When his father-in-law, Creon,
offers him the crown, Herakles denounces him as "public and
proud, constrained and crafty-wise." Herakles fears that to accept
worldly power would prevent him from finding his other-worldly
self, and he flees the court. In the street, he listens to the Poet's
song of the spirit and vows to escape from his own animality:

> Too well I know that I contain them all—
> The serpent, wolf and jackal, ape and cur,
> Lion and hog:—of old the beasts are laired
> In life's primeval wilderness, the dark,
> Trackless and devil-haunted waste within me! . . . . .
> Yet, in the mind's rapt outlook, I discern
> That in the jungle is the Householder,
> Whose patient labour has made room and home
> And let the light into his dwelling place!
> Now, while he sleeps, it may be, in his stead

Garrulous ghosts and fauns infest the gloom
And in his name accomplish shameful deeds,
Shallow and eloquent sincerities,
Profession of all faiths that falsify,
And threadbare fashions of a masquerade—
While from the teeming dark they snarl and whine,
Chatter and roar and laugh, gibber and grin
With greedy eyes and fangs—the beasts, the beasts
Who harbour where his realm is unreclaimed!.....
                                        (II, 219)

Herakles returns to his house and overhears his wife, Megara, singing a lullaby to their children. Megara, who represents the attractions of domesticity, counsels resignation to the cycle of birth and death. She sings to her children:

For yesterday is all we are,
    To-morrow all we yet shall be;
    The end is whence no eye can see......
We only know the way is far!

We only know men grow and grieve
    And die.....And death is strange and sore!
    O sleep, my darlings, sleep!—before
The time returns to wake—to live!
                                        (II, 228)

To Herakles, resignation implies an intolerable abdication of human spiritual potential. Aware of the "large light of life," he finds no guidance in the soothing maternal song; and he descends with his companion Iolaus into the human netherworld, represented by a tavern. "Here's still a last, least place / Where laughter is, where there is light and wine / And song," Herakles tells Iolaus. Herakles senses a kinship with the thieves and prostitutes in the tavern, and he realizes that their gaiety masks a spiritual despair. Beneath the "counterfeit" song of the tavern, he hears the silent "chaunt of the divine awakening":

There is a sound, a semblance as of song,
A quiver of rhythmic motion in the air.....
But then and still thereafter there is silence,
Strictly distinguished to the inward ear.
Hark—and your soul shall hear it as I do!

> They sing not—neither can they sing at all,
> Who are as we in bondage to this world!
> Their music is a shallow counterfeit,
> The unsubstantial echo of a voice;—
> Not the phrased splendour of essential song
> Rumoured along the surface of the soul's
> Deep seas of elemental harmony!.....
>
> (II, 249–50)

Without knowledge of it, Herakles has already begun to radiate in his demeanor the light within him; and the Woman, as she emerges from the tavern, instinctively recognizes him as the Redeemer. She begs to follow him; but Herakles insists that "There are no followers / Nor captains on the soul's eternal quest!" His plan to isolate himself to await a full revelation of self is thwarted by the arrival at court of a messenger from King Eurystheus.

Before Herakles goes to court to receive the message, he returns home to tell Megara of his newfound mission. Still deeply bound to domestic life, Herakles assumes that his family will share his quest:

> This is the loveliest and most bountiful
> Of all good fortune of man's mortal life:
> Surely it shall not for the truth's sake pass
> Out of the sum of real prosperities!
> Rather my loved ones and my love shall share,
> Always with me and to whatever end,
> The days and ways of the enfranchised soul!
>
>
> (II, 274–75)

Herakles is still ignorant of the horrible price of truth. Not only must he leave his loved ones for the sake of truth, but he must destroy them because they constantly lure him toward cowardly resignation.

Creon, who is Lodge's best-drawn exponent of skepticism and materialism, interprets Herakles' spiritual aspirations as a form of insanity. Because he believes that man's fate is sealed by blind cosmic forces, Creon chooses to approach life with urbane irony:

> Now, when the game of life is played—and lost,—
> Lost in the main, yet somehow hurried through
> To the calm, threadbare, tolerable end,—

> The humour of the thing comes quietly home,
> As we discern how wise we were to take
> The loss for granted—and enjoy the game!
> . . . .
> Yes! . . . . . he discerns, beyond his private fault
> And failure,—when the game is played, and lost,—
> Where thought turns sick and dizzy and dismayed
> On the black borders of its own abyss,—
> How all men living are not ever free,
> But straitly prisoned in the Mystery,
> Burdened beneath the universal strength,
> Merged in the flux of dark infinites.....
> Which are the Gods!—in whose relentless grasp
> The strong man strives and strangles and is slain.
>
> (II, 289–90)

The Poet, whose faith has been shaken by the night in the tavern, reaffirms it when he hears Creon's philosophy. The Poet rejects a posture of humorous detachment because it "seems like the simper on a dead man's face." While Creon confidently predicts that Herakles, like all strong men, will be crushed, the Poet hails him as the Redeemer.

When Herakles arrives at court, he rejects the message from Eurystheus, which orders him to perform the twelve labors. As the message implies, to perform "the tasks and toil of servitude" would force Herakles to sacrifice his quest for personal spirituality for the material benefit of the people. While the messenger warns him it is futile to resist, the Woman professes her faith in him. Torn between them, Herakles lashes out in anger against Eurystheus and rushes from court.

Herakles wanders through the streets, ashamed that when put to the test, he has lapsed into a rage more befitting a wounded animal than a would-be Redeemer. In the depths of his despair, he hears the people praying to their gods; and his sense of mission is rekindled by their slavish reverence:

> Pathos—humility—surrender—fear!—
> Starved, sterile, satisfied, supremely sad.
> Human vociferation and appeal!—
> O frightened children, crying in the dark!—
> Be well assured this hour of lamentation,
> Of weakness and despair shall pass away!

> Unconquerable is the strength within me—soon,
> Soon to revive!—and spares not, neither counts
> The cost!
>
> (II, 330–31)

But Herakles still does not understand how great the cost will be. He resists the truth when Teiresias prophesies to him:

> Most wretched of the sons of men
> Is he who breaks the bonds of human fate
> And dares the soul's transcendent destiny!
> . . . .
> For all his life is lost to save his life;
> And all he loved is sacrificed and slain
> To make love pure and perfect in his heart!—
>
> (II, 333)

Herakles refuses to believe the prophecy until he receives it directly from the oracle at Delphi. When he goes to Delphi, however, he rends the temple veil to find the sanctuary empty. Suddenly, he realizes that revelation as well as power to transcend his animality emanates from within his own soul:

> Coward and weak and abject!. . . . .O my Soul!—
> How long the dark persuasion of my fears
> Has wrought deception, and consoled the heart
> With lies of some conceivable escape!.....
> How long even I have dreamed false dreams of God,
> As of some other than the self I know,
> To whom might meanly, secretly be shifted
> The endless labour of the soul's perfection,
> The mystery of being, and the deep,
> Unuttered meaning of the Universe!.....
>
> (II, 357)

No longer will Herakles seek release from the suffering of the quest. In the ecstasy of vision he accepts at last the full cost of transcendence:

> I am resolved to death, to tears and blood,
> To desolation and intolerable

Bereavement,—to the worst that needs must be!
And to the best, to new nativities,
I am resolved! And I will stand apart,
Naked and perfect in my solitude,
Aloft in the clear light perpetually,—
Having afforded to the uttermost
The blood-stained, tear-drenched ransom of the soul!.....
                                        (II, 363–64)

The bloodstained ransom of the soul occurs in the tenth scene of *Herakles*, in which the drama of ideas suddenly turns to brutal action. When he returns home, Herakles recognizes that his bonds to his family cannot be broken without carnage. While his children scream for mercy, Herakles murders them. He collapses in a fit before he can kill Megara. Like Cain, Herakles acts out the logical insanity of the Conservative Christian Anarchist: murder for the sake of life, annihilation of the old self so that the new self may be born. Herakles, again like Cain, chants a hymn of rebirth in the words of Jesus:

I am the madman; and the murderer
I am; and I am Herakles; and I,
I am the Resurrection and the Life,
I am the Soul, whose inmost virtue is
Thus to outlive destruction and return,
Valid with Truth's perennial victory!—
                                        (II, 407)

Truth transcends all human morality and justifies what seems a heinous crime. To Megara, who cries for justice, Herakles says:

                    Truth is just.
And Truth prevails, relentless and revealed
Between us:—I, the living; you the lost.....
Only the soul survives—only the soul
Whose self and substance are the living truth!
Therefore am I redeemed.
                                        (II, 409)

The man-god has a responsibility, however, to lead his people out of slavery to false gods and into the freedom of truth. Thus Herakles accepts the labors of Eurystheus:

Therefore the Labours!—for the soul must strive,
The God must serve, until His virtue is,
In man's degraded being and abject heart,
In man's deformed, incurious, haunted mind,
In man's gross greed and dull brutalities,
Illustrious and exemplified!—till truth,
Loved and proclaimed, at last is lived and known!
(II, 420)

As Herakles departs, the Poet and the Woman join Herakles'
mother and wife in singing the praises of the Redeemer.
The final scene of *Herakles*, which, as Adams suggested, might be
read as a separate poem, concerns the final labor of Herakles—the
freeing of Prometheus. Herakles tells Prometheus that he has en-
dured his chains to no purpose, for the God whose powers Prometheus has defied does not exist:

Thus rose the myth of God, when time was young,
When, curious of whatever strictly shaped
The horror and hardship of his destiny,
Man's fear and ignorance conceived the cause
In his own likeness, and believed—and wept!
Now we have looked abroad and looked within,
Straining the symbol, and we learn to know,
Quietly and at last, its secret sense,
Shadowed and insufficiently set forth,
Is, in the meaning and the truth, ourselves!—
We are the Gods!
(II, 443)

The instant that Prometheus recognizes this truth, the chains fall
from his body, and he achieves full liberty, which is "the freedom to
become Free." Truth has destroyed Prometheus's ordered conception of the universe; and he asks Herakles, "Where are the labours
and the life?..... / Where is the conflict?.....Where the victory?....." In his reply, Herakles accepts Creon's vision of a chaotic universe; but, whereas Creon names the chaos "God" and sub-
mits to its power, Herakles upholds the power of the human mind to
forge order amid chaos:

Knowledge alone is victory! When all
Is understood, all is subdued, received,

> Possessed and perfect. For the soul of man
> Is, in the universe of force and change,
> Of blind, immeasurable energies,
> Subtile and secret and supremely one,
> The sole self-realized power, the single strength
> Aimed and reflective and perfectible.
> Therefore alone the mind's conception turns
> Chaos to cosmos, ignorance to truth,
> Force to the freedom of articulate laws—
> Giving to phases of the senseless flux,
> One after one, the soul's identity.
>
> (II, 453)

In this speech, Frederick Conner has perceived an echo of Hegel's *Phenomenology of Spirit,* in which "the Absolute Self comes to self-realization through a brutal but progressive dialectic at the end of which it knows itself in all-inclusive knowledge."[17] All of Lodge's work was informed by his knowledge of Hegel, Schopenhauer, and Nietzsche. However, in language this passage more closely resembles the final chapters of *The Education of Henry Adams,* which Lodge read while writing *Herakles,* and *The Rule of Phase Applied to History,* by which Lodge was so impressed that he asked for and received a personal copy of the manuscript. Adams's scientific theory of history attempted to measure "blind, immeasurable energies" by "articulate laws," and to distinguish "phases" in the "senseless flux." Ernest Samuels has suggested that *The Rule of Phase Applied to History* could be considered Adams's version of a Prometheus poem. Both Adams and Lodge desperately sought to turn chaos into cosmos, to impose order (whether mythic or scientistic) on a disordered universe. *Herakles* was not Lodge's last act of faith; but, during the final year of his life, he grew increasingly certain that his philosophy was falling on deaf ears.

CHAPTER 6

The Dark Shuts Down

A LFRED Kazin has called *The Education of Henry Adams* "a patrician's inside story of a dominant group, a leading class, an elite." In effect, Adams envisioned two audiences for *The Education:* the one hundred recipients of the 1907 private edition who would catch the ironies and nuances of the "inside story"; and the readers of the posthumous 1918 edition who would press their noses against the glass of Adams's world to find it impenetrable. By writing for a select few, Kazin argues, Adams freed himself from inhibitions: "This concern for effect on a few immediate listeners is the psychological driving power of the *Education.* During his life Henry Adams did not have a large audience and could not have wanted one. But he turned this lack . . . into a way of imposing himself on his own distinguished circle, dominating this 'inside ring' by the speculative freedom of his talk."[1]

George Cabot Lodge, who received a copy of the private edition, imagined the audience for *Herakles* in similar terms. "You know that I write for myself, of course, and then, as things are in fact, just for you and so few others," Lodge told Marjorie Nott. "You'll find it [*Herakles*], of course, long; and you'll strike, I guess, sandy places. Perhaps, though, there are some secrets in it and some liberties."[2] Having failed to reach either a popular audience or the educated public, Lodge deliberately wrote *Herakles* for his own "inside ring." Lodge sent the poem to about sixty readers whom he felt would understand its secrets and liberties. When this limited audience had reservations about *Herakles*, Lodge, with a growing sense of failure and isolation, resigned himself to "singing in a vacuum." Ironically, from the depths of Lodge's hopelessness emerged his best late poem, "The Noctambulist."

I *Reactions to* Herakles

After Bernard Berenson read his presentation copy of *Herakles*, he asked the opinion of his friend Robert Calverley Trevelyan. In a long, detailed letter Trevelyan, a classicist and poet, judged the poem powerful but greatly flawed:

It would be easy enough to find fault, in fact there is hardly any fault he has not committed. And yet the poem interested me very much, and because of its merits, I think, not because of its faults. I think some of the main conceptions, though seldom treated adequately, are really fine. Undramatic as the poem is in form and method, his idea of Heracles' psychology is magnificently dramatic if only he had carried it out dramatically. It seems to me that a great deal of the trouble arises from the impossible form he has chosen. If one sets about writing a play which is not intended to be acted, one ought not to consider that an excuse for making it move ten times as slow as an ordinary acting play, and allowing the characters to repeat all their ideas and phrases at least ten times, which is pretty much what he does. And yet at moments, as when Heracles kills his children, he makes one think he has a great deal of dramatic imagination, if it were not continually swamped in endless bogs of rather crude quasi-philosophy. . . . Well, I really do not know what to think about it. He has considerable powers of expression, and a great deal, only too much, fluency; but I do not feel that he has much sense of style yet, except sometimes when dramatically inspired. . . . It is something considerable to have conceived and carved out a big theme like that, full of generous ideas, even if only partially successful in executing it. You asked me to say what I thought, so I have done my best: but it is rather a puzzle.[3]

Berenson sent Trevelyan's criticisms to Adams, who in turn showed them to Lodge. "You seem, at first glance, to have knocked your poor Britisher rather groggy," Adams told him.[4] Trevelyan's response, which on the whole was perceptive and fair, greatly disappointed Lodge.

Yet Trevelyan articulated the misgivings about *Herakles* that those closer to Lodge tactfully implied in their restrained approval. Adams himself had reacted rather groggily: "The Heracles strikes me as so big a thing I hesitate to say what I think about it. You must give me time. Your ambition is vast, that you should begin by Aeschylus and Shelley and God knows who else, challenging them all to a contest, as though we were still Athenians of B.C. 500, and you were the youthful Sophocles. We are certainly not Athenians, and if Sophocles or Aeschylus were alive in you, we should never know it."[5] Brooks Adams carefully remained neutral: "It is a great attempt that you have made, and time alone can test your success. . . . Frankly I must admit that I have doubts as to your philosophy, but the literary excellence of a book has nothing to do with philosophy. There can be no doubt of the power of your conception, and some of the songs have very great tenderness and charm."[6]

S. Weir Mitchell also reacted cautiously: "It is interesting—Few long poems are—It has noble & eloquent passages—Rememberable lines,—freshness of phrases, now & then lingual surprises . . . and my loved lyric verses—some of it most satisfying."[7] Edith Wharton criticized the poem more explicitly but softened her words in equivocation: "There is some splendid poetry in it. . . . My chief criticism, on a first reading, is that Herakles perhaps repeats himself, not in words, of course, but in thought; & that this gives, here & there, a static quality to the poem. But I may be wrong.—"[8] These readers at least finished *Herakles.* One friend wrote to Lodge that he admired the "nobility" of the first six scenes, as if to say he had read no farther. Henry James promised to "dip into it," but he complained of his chronic aversion to dramatic poetry.[9]

Lodge considered *Herakles* his masterpiece, the culmination of his career, that his "inside ring" could generate only halfhearted enthusiasm for it hurt Lodge deeply. The few reviews of *Herakles* only confirmed his sense of defeat. The *Harvard Graduates Magazine* praised his blank verse but concluded, "We feel, nevertheless, that his Herakles lacks vitality."[10] The *New York Times* remarked, "Here also is the smell of the academic lamp. The blank verse moves with dignity, but the poet is stirred by memories of Hellenic legends, not by life."[11] Although some Boston newspapers had kind words for *Herakles,* the only favorable review in a national publication did not appear until the month of Lodge's death.[12] By then, it was too late, for Lodge had already convinced himself that no audience, however small, existed for his poetry.

If Lodge had intended *Herakles* solely for his friends, he probably would have prevented its public sale. That more than two hundred copies of the first edition were made available to the public indicates that Lodge harbored faint hopes of public recognition. Ironically, this book, the most private of his works, became the first to go into a second edition, an event that gratified Lodge. However, the public response resembled at times a parody of the approval Lodge sought, for *Herakles* seemed to appeal to a literary fringe element. One reader, who identified herself to Lodge as THE COSMIC WOMAN, offered to grasp his hand in "*Understanding!*" She proclaimed that *Herakles* transcended literature to become Truth itself. Four years after Lodge's death, *Herakles* inspired a sophomore at Columbia to undertake a dramatic symposium among Byron, Shelley, and Lodge. As the author confided to Henry Cabot Lodge, the conversation was to take place in Hades after the poet-heroes had visited the upper world.

Perhaps bewildered by THE COSMIC WOMAN, Lodge distrusted at first the enthusiastic praise of the Reverend Alfred H. Brown, who wrote, "Your soul lives, and has stood, like Herakles, upon the Crag of Caucasus above the human Prometheus, bound in the chains of conventions, ignorance, and fear. You have sounded the new (old) gospel of redemption, the one great Truth—'I am.' . . . 'Herakles' is the greatest spiritual poem I have read in American Literature. It is tremendously true. Yours in the divinity of man."[13] Lodge sent the letter to Adams, who concluded, "He has some glimmer of intelligence, has Brown; therefore I take him to be a crank. Tant Mieux!"[14] Brown had abandoned the pulpit to lecture on modern drama in Boston, and he told Lodge that he wanted to teach *Herakles* in his course.

Herakles had gone into a second printing, but, as Lodge realized, largely because of Brown's promoting it among his friends and assigning it to his students. In July, 1909, Lodge wrote to Adams of his solitude, "I find suddenly that one ends by wanting someone to take an interest—which alarms me a little, because it's so obvious that no one will."[15] Brown seemed to be the exception that proved the rule, and Lodge described to Adams an awkward meeting with his would-be disciple:

I had taken for granted that he would be sloppy & dreadful, & it was with an odd sensation of relief that I found he wasn't at all, but, on the contrary, quite sane & really intelligent & full of enthusiasm for "Herakles." Well, I didn't quite know how to behave, never having had such an experience before. . . . I wooed & caressed him, of course, & of course I prize him more than gold; but I find, nevertheless, that Brown's solitary figure does not materially relieve the austerity of my situation. From her deserted altars my goddess still utters her imperishable oracles, and I still try to set them down in song; but I can't help reflecting that all the world is in the Valley below watching the baseball game.[16]

If he had no audience, Lodge recognized that the situation resulted to some extent from his own choice. "I complain," he told Marjorie Nott, "of the usual, &, I suppose, for a man like me, inevitable situation, for which I glory to acknowledge my entire & sole responsibility, and of course I wouldn't change anything essential if I could. Persons living on the frontiers have always, I imagine, been obliged to do all their own work."[17] This statement contains a crucial fact overlooked by those who have attributed Lodge's failure as a poet entirely to the "stifling atmosphere" of his society. Such a view portrays Lodge as a totally passive victim when, through his conscious withdrawal from society, Lodge contributed actively to his own fate.

For Lodge, alienation was as much a precondition as a consequence of his poetry. In "Mediocracy," Henry Everard asks himself whether he has used public neglect of his work as a rationalization for his own failure. Everard decides conclusively that the fault lies with society and not with his art. Lodge was never so sure, and he was torn between contempt for the reading public and self-contempt for failing to reach that audience. At times, he wanted desperately to immerse himself in the conventional life of his era as his father and his ancestors had done. At other times, he yearned for the escape of the contemplative life, symbolized by Tuckernuck Island. His acute sense of alienation pervaded his last poem, "The Noctambulist."

II "*The Noctambulist*"

In "The Noctambulist," which was inspired in part by E. A. Robinson's "Captain Craig," Lodge explored the meaning of his isolation from the world. The young narrator of the poem relates his conversation with a haunted old man, whose life reflects what Lodge felt his own life had become. In a dim tavern, across a table lit by a solitary candle, the old man tells the youth and his female companion of his younger days:

> "I know!...O Youth!...I too have seen the world
> At sunrise, candid as the candid dew;
> And felt, responsive to the cosmic life,
> My senses kindle and my veins abound,—

My life leap forward like an eager flame!"
. . . .
                                          "I have been," he said,
"Since I was young like you—as once I was!—
Round and about this little, day-lit world,
And drained its springs of wisdom!—And to you,
Who'll not believe me,—since no man is spared
His journey round the world, and from the Springs
No drop can pass to quench another's thirst,—
I'll tell the ancient, ill-considered truth:
Wisdom's a shallow source, and all the world
Is near and small! Yes! the one soul within
Contains them all and yearns unsatisfied..."
                                          (II, 142–44)

In his youth, the old man followed the path of idealism, confident
of finding truth. He tore down the effigies of false gods, experienced
the power of love, and preached his vision to the world. As the years
passed, however, he slowly recognized that it was hopeless to try to
reform the world. He has resolved, therefore,

                                          "To wage no more
With phantoms of the past fortunate wars;
To die no longer on the barricades
For the true faith; to spend no more the rich
And insufficient days and powers of life
Striving to shape the world and force the facts,
Tame the strong heart and stultify the soul,
To fit some creed, some purpose, some design
Ingeniously contrived to spare the weak,
Protect the timid and delude the fools,—
Who feel no deep, inspired response to life's
Whole power and peril;—and to beautify
By nice discrimination,—to explain
By phrase and fraud and fancy,—to reform
By dint of gross damnations and a most
Robust stupidity!"
                                          (II, 147)

Having renounced the world and the daylight of the world's
"wisdom," The Noctambulist embraces the "illimitable Night" of his
alienation. Like Cain and Herakles, he knows that the quest for
transcendence must be made alone, and in the dark:

> "Only the Night is best—the Night wherein
> Our eyes, long-used and wearied with the gross
> World's inconsiderable spectacle,
> Grow spacious, and, no longer blind with sun,
> See, in the incommensurable dark,
> Sudden as song, above, beyond us—stars!..."
>
> (II, 149)

While the slaves of convention lead their meaningless lives, the Noctambulist seeks his divine identity:

>   "Now I watch
> You turn and turn in the same beaten track
> Of brief desires and strict necessities,
> While from the thronged vast circus round about
> Stare down upon you all the eyes of the world
> Which crowns the victor and vanquished scorns!
> And thus, or well or ill, you run your race,
> Going no-whither tho' the prize be won...
> I know!—I ran once—and at last o'er-ran
> My shadow!—Yes!—and so, abruptly paused,
> Torn with tremendous laughter and wild tears,
> Feeling truth's silent and relentless scorn,
> Flame-edged, of all I was and all my deeds;
> And set upon by the derisive shout
> And fear and anger of the world, I broke
> The circus walls, and hastily passed on.
> And found the Darkness everywhere, and saw,
> Thereafter, certain stars!...And now, at least
> I go no more the dull, determined rounds,
> Like a tame squirrel whirling in its cage!
> I'm a Noctambulist: and in the Night
> The star-traced, trackless ways return no more...."
>
> (II, 150–51)

As the Noctambulist fades into the darkness to resume his endless search for truth and light, the youth recognizes his own cowardice and unworthiness:

> We heard his footfall on the vacant stair
> The whole night long. We lay awake in bed
> And heard him climb;—but those who slept instead

> Smiled and assured us that he was not there.
> We had our own important things to care
> About—the place, profit and the daily bread;
> And then the street so thundered in one's head...
> And often life's a commonplace affair!
> Yet then we heard him!—we not they were right:
> We heard him—Yes! tho' now we sleep by night
> Almost as soundly as we sleep by day,
> We waked, we heard him, heard—and nothing more....
> For we, inert as they who heard not, lay
> Damned and dishonoured as he passed our door!
>
> (II, 152)

The youth has "made with life the needful compromise" (II, 153). Too weak or too comfortable, the youth cannot step into the darkness with the Noctambulist to seek "new powers of the imperishable mind" (II, 154).

Lodge considered "The Noctambulist" a "really new and large and valid departure" in his poetry.[18] He used a semidramatic form he had invented during the winter of 1908–09—a blank-verse poem with a coda of three sonnets that summarize and intensify the themes of the blank-verse section. "The Noctambulist" represents Lodge's highest development of this promising form that allowed him to combine in one poem the lyric and dramatic modes. "The Noctambulist" marked a departure for Lodge in language as well as in form. Vestiges of inflated diction remain in the poem, but in general the language is simpler and the metaphors more concrete than in his earlier work.

Unfortunately, the same cannot be said for most of *The Soul's Inheritance and Other Poems*, the volume Lodge was preparing when he died and that appeared posthumously in 1909. In *The Soul's Inheritance* Lodge collected several of his shorter poems, written after *The Great Adventure;* and he recast them in the blank-verse and sonnet form of "The Noctambulist." Tedious variations on Lodge's persistent theme of transcendence, these poems lack the dramatic form and the sober perspective on the transcendental quest that distinguish "The Noctambulist."

Lodge seems to have organized the volume to reflect his tempered vision; the vibrantly optimistic poems lead up to "The Noctambulist." But Lodge ended the book by reasserting the need for "Faith":

> Hourly to find perfection in all things,
> And in ourselves perfection;—day by day,
> Greatly adventured on the endless way,
> To realize truth's inspired imaginings;—
> To beat up the wide skies of thought on wings
> Radiant with sunrise;—to depart away
> Into the future with the great grave gay
> Passionate heart of life that loves and sings;—
> This is the soul's desire!—the secret aim
> Of life's dim aspiration, from the sod
> Thro' countless forms, thro' beast and man and God!—
> This is the mind's pure ecstasy; and this
> Is love, which kindles to a single flame
> Life's immemorial validities!

> > (II, 159)

When *Poems and Dramas of George Cabot Lodge* was published in 1911, Lodge's father grouped five uncollected poems with those of *The Soul's Inheritance*, thereby obscuring the thematic structure of the volume. However, these appended poems, particularly "Ilion" and "Lower New York," were among Lodge's best.

Like Wordsworth, Lodge had once awaited the dawn on Westminster Bridge, and "Lower New York" was his rejoinder to Wordsworth's famous sonnet. Full of wonder at the beauty of the sleeping city, Wordsworth had written, "Dull would he be of soul who could pass by / A sight so touching in its majesty."[19] The ships, towers, domes, theaters, and temples seemed to blend into the fields and sky; the City and Nature fused, "All bright and glittering in the smokeless air." Wordsworth concluded:

> N'er saw I, never felt, a calm so deep!
> The river glideth at his own sweet will:
> Dear God! the very houses seem asleep;
> And all that mighty heart is lying still!

For Lodge, the deep calm of the city at dawn has become the coma of "a vast necropolis of souls":

> Here is the dawn a hopeless thing to see:
> Sordid and pale as is the face of one
> Who sinks exhausted in oblivion
> After a night of deep debauchery.

> > (II, 168)

Anesthetized by "sordid greed and passions mean and blind," the
inhabitants of the city rise to begin their "dull, dreadful labour" at
the "court and prison, warehouse and exchange." Like the crowd
that flows over London Bridge in Eliot's *The Waste Land*, Lodge's
city dwellers seem "more dead than death"; their lives are "aimless
and empty as an idiot's mind."

As Monroe K. Spears has said, the modern city, especially as it
approaches the condition of an Infernal City, is "the environment
and scene, and hence a part of the subject" of much Modernist
poetry.[20] If in "The Noctambulist" Lodge seemed to be approaching
the   dramatic   and   semidramatic   forms   of   more   successful
contemporaries like Robinson and Robert Frost, he seemed in
"Lower New York" to be anticipating the ironic tone and squalid
urban settings of Eliot and Pound. It is idle to speculate about the
direction of Lodge's work, had he lived longer; but it is possible that
the Imagist Movement, barely stirring in 1909, might have provided
Lodge with a fresh poetics and thus have allowed him to escape the
poetic genteel tradition. Tragically, Lodge had no chance to fulfill
his promise.

III   *The Jumping-off Place*

In July, 1909, Lodge and Mitchell sailed to Tuckernuck for a
ten-day vacation. Mitchell had not visited the island since 1903, and
Lodge's spirits soared in the company of his friend. He assured his
mother that he was "getting, daily, into splendid shape, mental &
physical."[21] Mitchell was encouraged by Lodge's apparent good
health, but he feared that Lodge would return too quickly to a
strenuous regimen of writing.

After a brief stay at Nahant, Lodge returned to the island in
August with his father to await the arrival of Bigelow from Paris.
Four days later he wrote to Bigelow, "I read a good deal, and take
my swim, and an occasional sail. Also, after a month's vacation
during which I haven't written a line, I've now begun again, and
write and meditate for four or five hours every day . . . so that life
flows evenly and quietly and cheerfully."[22] This was Lodge's last
letter. Despite his protestations of vigor, he must have sensed that
the end was close; for he had suffered during the summer several
mild heart attacks that the family had innocently interpreted as
indigestion.

On August 19, the Reverend Alfred H. Brown arrived for lunch, carrying an article he had just completed on Lodge's work. Delighted by Brown's interest and intelligence, Lodge told him, "Nobody ever understood my poems so well before."[23] That night Lodge contracted ptomaine poisoning from eating a bad clam, and acute nausea racked him until dawn. During the next day, he seemed to improve; he ate lightly and managed to sleep. By nine that evening, the nausea recurred, accompanied by shortness of breath. His father, now greatly alarmed, sent to Nantucket for a doctor. On the morning of August 21, the doctor examined Lodge and found that the sickness had seriously weakened his heart. He administered alternate injections of glycerine and digitalis throughout the day, but Lodge remained in danger. Toward evening, the doctor advised Senator Lodge to summon the family. Shortly after ten o'clock, Lodge died in his father's arms. A few days later, when Elizabeth and John Ellerton Lodge rowed to the deep water off Nahant, Elizabeth carried her husband's remains in the Greek vase Stickney had given them for a wedding present. As Bay had requested, Elizabeth cast the vase into the sea.

Lodge's sudden death crushed those closest to him. The depth of personal loss reflected in their letters of condolence documented Lodge's profound impact on each of them. As Elizabeth Cameron said, "It seems to me that the measure of Bay is the hole he leaves in so many lives—a space that can never be filled for any of us."[24] The others concurred. To his friends, Lodge represented youth and hope and joy. His presence, more than his poetry, manifested the transcendental vision that was the goal of his life and work. Those who knew him, including some of the most brilliant people of the time, considered George Cabot Lodge to be a truly extraordinary man. Those who can glimpse his charismatic presence only in refractions might agree with a reader of Edith Wharton's article about Lodge: "The man must have had a sort of aura about him. Perhaps he was one of those who walk on the outer rim of the world, aware of the jumping-off place; which seems the only way to walk,—but few take it."[25]

CHAPTER 7

Lodge in American Literary History

HENRY Cabot Lodge, in grief for his son, vowed to devote the remainder of his life to hastening George Cabot Lodge's literary recognition. "All my ambition's long since burned out," he told Bigelow, "but now I want to live and keep my health while I can, because I can be of use to his wife and children; and I want also to rear the monument,—to bring out his poems, which have crept without notice into the world, in a collected edition. . . . He has written poems that will live, that will take their place in the great annals of English verse and human thought. I want to see him recognized, and I think we shall, even in the few years that may remain to us."[1] Lodge repeated this hope over and over again in letters to his friends,[2] and he grasped in the following years every opportunity to advance his son's reputation. But even by the time of Senator Lodge's death in 1924, the work of George Cabot Lodge had passed behind a cloud of neglect from which it has never emerged.

I *Lodge's Literary Reputation*

Almost immediately after Lodge's death, Edith Wharton expressed to his widow her desire to write a tribute to him. Henry Cabot Lodge eagerly accepted Wharton's offer and urged her to publish her essay in *Scribner's*, where it appeared in February, 1910. "It would be impossible, I think, for any friend of George Cabot Lodge's to write of the poet without first speaking of the man," Wharton began. She had loved the man more than his verse, and her essay focused on the poetry only so far as it reflected him. Passing in tactful generalities over Lodge's early volumes, she reserved her praise for *Herakles* and for some of the posthumously published lyrics and sonnets. She noted Lodge's increasing mastery over dramatic forms, and his movement at the end of his career

116

toward more concrete imagery. "The Noctambulist" she called "perhaps the completest product" of his art.[3] Wharton feared that the detached tone of her article and its emphasis on the later poetry might offend the Lodges, but they were delighted with the essay, as they were with the almost simultaneous appearance of a glowing review of *The Soul's Inheritance* in the *Chicago Tribune* and of Alfred Brown's article in *Twentieth Century Magazine*.

In the exuberant style of his letters to Lodge, Brown claimed that Lodge had, "in a few years, made three contributions of unusual value to the treasury of American poetry, in addition to the meritorious volumes which he had previously published."[4] Brown, stressing Lodge's philosophy, dealt at length with *Cain, The Great Adventure*, and *Herakles*. Although he demonstrated a thorough knowledge of Lodge's poetry and a keen sensitivity to his subject's ideas, Brown lacked Wharton's judicious tone.

By the spring of 1910, Henry Cabot Lodge had assembled the contents of the proposed collected works, and he asked Theodore Roosevelt to write a preface and Henry Adams to write a biography as the third volume of the set. Roosevelt, warming to the task, declared in the preface, "Of all the men with whom I have been intimately thrown he was the man to whom I would apply the rare name of genius." Roosevelt lavishly praised Lodge's intelligence, scholarly accomplishments, and poetic aspirations. Comparing his friend to the great poet-soldiers of history—Cervantes and Philip Sidney—Roosevelt depicted Lodge as a man standing on life's crest, "his veins thrilling with eager desire, his eyes fronting the future with dauntless and confident hope."[5]

Adams undertook his biography with considerably less enthusiasm. He had refused in 1905 to write a biography of John Hay for fear of Mrs. Hay's censorial meddling, and he expected the Lodges, despite their good intentions, to interfere similarly. "Poor Bay's poems are to be republished in a collected form," he wrote to Elizabeth Cameron. "Bessy [Elizabeth Lodge] wants me to do a volume of Life. I assent readily, knowing that Cabot [Henry Cabot Lodge] will do it, and will not let anyone else do it, however he may try to leave it alone."[6] Adams gathered Lodge's letters and manuscripts before sailing to Paris in April, 1910. After completing half the biography in May, he complained to Mrs. Cameron that he could "make nothing very good out of it."[7] Nevertheless, in October he presented a draft to the family for approval.

As Adams had predicted, the Lodges complicated the project. Elizabeth submitted passages from Lodge's love letters for use in the book but later withdrew them as too personal. Senator Lodge caviled over genealogical details. Despite the pessimistic late poems, Mrs. Lodge insisted on the deletion of all "reference to failing health or discouragement," and she did so on the grounds that her son "wanted & meant to appear at least adequate & cheerful to the world."[8] Adams made it clear, however, that responsibility for all suppressions or changes must lie with the family. "As for the MS.," he warned Elizabeth Lodge, "it was sent to you to do what you pleased with it. That is your part of the work, with which I have nothing to do. From the moment the MS. comes into your hands, it ceases to be mine and is wholly yours."[9]

However, the major reason for Adams's uneasiness in writing *The Life of Lodge* was not family disagreement over its content, but what he perceived as the essential hypocrisy of the biography. "Bay liked his Boston even less than I do," he reminded Elizabeth, "and we shall have trouble in trying to make this clear without using some of his own strong expressions. I foresee constant stumbling over this potato-patch; all the more because it is really the gist of the poetry. All the poems express a more or less violent reaction against Boston, and ought to be read so, if they are to be understood."[10] Of course, Henry Cabot Lodge intended the collected works and the companion biography precisely for the Boston audience that his son had rejected. Adams, frustrated that he could not write the iconoclastic book that he and Lodge would have wanted, resorted to stylistic subterfuge. He would attack Boston by indirection, as he explained to Elizabeth:

In this society made up of forms of social cowardice, we must do as Bay did,—insist on recognition,—or submit to be swamped. In this last case, we had better leave biography alone. Bay would be ashamed of us, and I should be ashamed of myself, if we deserted his standards; and the highest standard he had was you.

Yet I have so far respected the so-called American standards of taste, which are mere standards of feebleness, as to tone down the expression of my own standards to a level which seems to me flat and cold. That is not the way I should express myself if I had only myself to express. It is not the way Bay expressed himself—I can only hope that, underneath the outside form of expression, the intensity of feeling will be unconsciously there, so as to affect the average idiot without his knowing it.[11]

This letter clarifies the curious tone of *The Life of Lodge;* it is so ironic at times that, as Edmund Wilson has observed, Adams "turns the poor young man into a shadow, and withers up his verse in a wintry pinch."[12] Adams tried deliberately to remove from the biography any trace of his intimate connection with and influence over Lodge. "My share in it is only to satisfy you and Bay," he wrote to Elizabeth; "and if I have allowed even a shadow of myself to come between him and his readers, I have made a mistake somewhere. I ought to be invisible; a mere mirror or . . . a slight tone of color."[13]

Adams had previously admonished Elizabeth that, "if one is a poet, or a poet's wife, or mother, one should be prepared to stand up to one's role, even in Boston!"[14] Adams recognized, however, that the Lodges would ensure that the book respected Bostonian canons of decorum; and he washed his hands of the affair. "So Cabot came to dinner last night to talk about Bay's publication," he wrote to Mrs. Cameron; "and of course I was beautiful and approved everything, and said that I agreed with everybody, which I always do because nobody cares. Sometimes I do it once too much, as in the case of John Hay's *Letters.* Bay's will be another case of the same sort, but not so lurid. If they will only let me keep my name off it!"[15] In fact, Adams arranged to delete his name from the title page on the pretext that it might distract the reader's attention from Lodge. He explained to Houghton Mifflin Company, "I prefer a very simple—simplest, title-page without anything that does not compel the public to think of the subject alone. For this reason I want to omit the author's name on the title, and rather insert it on the false title in front."[16] *The Life of George Cabot Lodge* was set in type in April, 1911, but its publication was delayed in order to coincide with the October issue of *Poems and Dramas of George Cabot Lodge.* Adams, in disgust, refused to think further of it. "I've made no special secret of my views about it," he told Mrs. Cameron, "but I don't want myself discussed."[17]

The literary press greeted *Poems and Dramas* warmly. "It is a brilliant achievement which is here embodied and commemorated," announced the *Dial.*[18] Other reviews were more measured in their praise but generally favorable. The *Nation* said: "While Lodge was not a great original poet, while his poetry may lack the consecration of genius, it has talent and character; while it may not make tradition, it is itself in the best literary tradition."[19] Although the *Literary Digest* called the sonnet "Cor Cordium" a "perfect poem," it

concluded that "the reader has to think his way through these books
. . . for Lodge never received that priceless gift of literary art, a
simple, clear, understandable style."[20] In the *Independent*, James
Herbert Morse deplored the derivative quality of Lodge's early
work, but he judged *Cain* to be "a great, strong, passionate, tho'
unactable drama."[21] Calling Lodge "a New England Swinburne,"
the *New York Times* praised his lyrics of love and nature but found
Herakles "a bore."[22]

Sending copies of Lodge's poems to those who evinced the
slightest interest in them, Senator Lodge, in the years after *Poems
and Dramas*, tried to keep his son's reputation alive. In 1912, during
a visit to Washington, John Galsworthy was presented with *Poems
and Dramas* by Lodge. Galsworthy was sufficiently impressed to
arrange the publication of an English edition by his own publisher,
William Heinemann.

In 1913, Professor P. C. Pavolini was introduced to *Herakles* by
his friend Bernard Berenson; and, with the encouragement of Berenson and Edith Wharton, he published a laudatory article in *Il
Marzocco*, a distinguished literary journal in Florence, Italy. Henry
Cabot Lodge quickly arranged a translation of the article and per-
suaded the editor of the *Living Age* to print it. "Are there in Italy six
persons who know the name of Lodge?" Pavolini asked. "It is very
doubtful if there are so many and this is not surprising when one
considers that in his own country he is hardly less unknown." Emphasizing the oriental elements in Lodge's philosophy, Pavolini presented a long explication of *Herakles*, which he called "a masterpiece." "The form is all Mr. Lodge's own: the brilliancy of
imagination, the terseness of expression, the statuesque lines, the
ineffable harmony of the verse."[23]

In 1915, Henry Cabot Lodge sent *Poems and Dramas* to James
Gibbons Huneker, whom young Lodge had met in Paris in 1896.
Huneker replied, "I have literally spent the week with his spirit and
. . . I may say that I rose exalted from each reading. We, America,
have lost our most promising poet. . . . It is only with the measuring
rod of the mightiest that you can gauge George Cabot Lodge."[24]
Huneker publically repeated his opinion in one of his newspaper
columns in October, 1918: "Among the younger American poets I
find one of genuine importance, not alone because of his poten-
tialities, but because of his actual performance. . . . Lodge had
assimilated a half dozen cultures, and had passed far out to sea the
perilous rocks of imitation upon which so many lesser talents have

come to grief." Huneker concluded, "He had the lyric art and also the architectural. He was a singer and a builder of the lofty rhyme."[25]

In 1916, in return for a presentation copy of *The Man Against the Sky*, Henry Cabot Lodge sent *Poems and Dramas* to E. A. Robinson. Robinson, who had been at Harvard during George Cabot Lodge's first two years, had never met him nor read his poetry before; but, having read the collection with "a combined sense of pleasure and discovery," he wrote:

> What I like best in his work is a certain uniformity of power and a kind of large spontaneity which I do not find in many,—I might almost say in any,—of our later writers. When I add that Moody had it, the list seems to be almost complete. I fancy that you will not disagree with me to any great extent when I tell you that I find in Herakles the best expression of the author's genius, which seems to me undeniable, although there is much to arouse one's genuine enthusiasm in Cain and many of the shorter poems. Many of the sonnets are magnificent, and a singularly happy effect is produced by the concluding sonnets which form a part of some of the longer poems in blank verse. One of the best examples of what I mean is the original and rather ominous piece called the Noctambulist. In fact, I should hardly hesitate to call this unusual combination the discovery of a new form in poetry, and a most effective one. I will not attempt to go through the books for examples of special excellence, for I should find too many titles to set down; and fearing that you may think my praise seems indiscriminate I will say frankly that there are times when poetry seems in these volumes to be confounded with rhetoric; but as this might be said with equal truth of all poets who have done sustained work in the grand style, I don't feel that I am discovering or announcing anything very disastrous. Herakles is undoubtedly one of the most significant poems of modern times. If its recognition continues to be slow, this slowness would not be from any lack of poetic value but from the fact that many readers would not accept its philosophy. I don't see how such work can be forgotten.[26]

Robinson rarely criticized the work of his contemporaries, and his feelings for Lodge's poetry were decidedly mixed. He tempered his praise with one telling criticism, characteristically understated: "There are times when poetry seems . . . to be confounded with rhetoric." Out of respect for Henry Cabot Lodge and for the tragic death of his son, Robinson probably minimized Lodge's weaknesses. Nevertheless, the remarkably positive statements cannot be completely discounted.

The availability of Lodge's poetry decreased gradually during the

1920s as his volumes went out of print; and his reputation, never firmly established despite his father's efforts, quickly faded. Henry Cabot Lodge had feared as early as 1919 that his son's recognition would not come as he had hoped. In that year William Lyon Phelps, one of the reigning academic arbiters of taste, published a history of twentieth-century poetry that ignored George Cabot Lodge. Senator Lodge was outraged, but Phelps's omission foreshadowed George Cabot Lodge's ensuing obscurity.

No significant anthology of American poetry has ever included more than two Lodge poems; most have left him out. Between J. G. Huneker's article in 1918 and 1940, Lodge's work received hardly a word of consideration. In 1940, Van Wyck Brooks revived Lodge briefly only to dismiss him as one of the "epigoni" of an exhausted literary tradition.[27] In their influential *History of American Poetry* (1946), Horace Gregory and Marya Zaturenska complained, "However hard we may try to discover actual poems in the memorial edition . . . the effort fails. . . . Lodge lacked the wit and the power to discover his own language. . . . His verse was imitative, restless, 'sad, bewildered,' and he seemed to look forward with the gaze of an adolescent into a hazy, 'larger, lovelier unknown heaven beyond the known!' "[28] Lodge's name was never mentioned in the massive two volumes of *Literary History of the United States* (1948). Louise Bogan in *Achievement in American Poetry* (1951) found Lodge "characterized more by young energy than by any sureness of idiom."[29] More recent studies of American poetry by Roy Harvey Pearce and by Hyatt H. Waggoner have altogether ignored Lodge.

This discrepancy between the enthusiasm for Lodge's work among some of his contemporaries and the relative antipathy of recent critics is partially explained by the enormous shift in taste since Lodge's death in 1909. Since in both form and content Lodge's verse runs counter to Modernist poetry, it can be approached fairly only if current assumptions about poetry are tempered with an understanding of Lodge's now antiquated poetics. He belonged to a transitional generation of poets, and his work fused the forms and themes of the nineteenth-century New England tradition with the tone of disillusionment so characteristic of twentieth-century poetry.

The period in American poetry from 1885 to 1912, called the "Twilight Interval" by E. C. Stedman,[30] has been singularly neglected in literary studies. The major figures, of course, have been properly examined, but no thorough attempt has ever been made to distinguish the respectable minor poetry of this period from the magazine verse that has mercifully passed into oblivion. Since minor poetry has a certain value in and of itself, and since it illuminates by contrast truly great poetry, Lodge's work may be seen to have a value similar to that of Jones Very, F. G. Tuckerman, George Henry Boker, or several minor figures from other periods who have received their due recognition.

Aside from the intrinsic merit of Lodge's finest poetry, his career has important implications for American literary history. Along with William Vaughn Moody and Trumbull Stickney, Lodge has usually been categorized as a Harvard Poet—as one of a tragic generation of writers who died before fulfilling their potential. Their early deaths have been interpreted as almost literal proof of a stifling atmosphere in their culture that made men like Lodge alienated persons. The idea of the alienated artist was firmly rooted in the Romantic movements of the nineteenth century; in the twentieth century, however, it has become a fundamental assumption of American literary history. Because George Cabot Lodge has been used as an example of the alienated artist in America, it is appropriate to examine the origin and propagation of this interpretation.

II *The Stifling Atmosphere*

The seminal interpretation of Lodge as victim of a stifling cultural atmosphere is Henry Adams's *Life of George Cabot Lodge*, which, as George Hochfield has said, "is perhaps the first American work of criticism to take as its motivating idea the inescapable alienation of the artist from society, and it represents that alienation as the cause of the unfullfillment and failure of the artist."[31] In the context of Adams's late work—*The Rule of Phase Applied to History* and *A Letter to American Teachers of History*—*The Life of Lodge* might be read as another scientistic application of the notion of entropy. In the first chapter of *The Life of Lodge*, Adams depicted a Boston whose cultural energy had been exhausted: "A poet, born in Boston, in 1873, saw about him, a society which commonly bred refined tastes, and often did refined work, but seldom betrayed strong emotions. The excitements of war had long passed; its ideals were forgotten, and no other great ideal had followed."[32] The poetic generation of Emerson, Holmes, and Lowell was dead or dying; and young Lodge cultivated his talent in an atmosphere devoid of "the classic and promiscuous turmoil of the forum, the theatre, or the bath, which trained the Greeks and the Romans, or the narrower contact of the church and the coffee-house, which bred the polished standards of Dryden and Racine" (7–8). Adams ironically assumed that Lodge's poetic aptitude must have been innate and not acquired because Boston "could not have inspired a taste for poetry" (7). In these circumstances, it was not surprising that Lodge, like Adams, should have developed an early antipathy to Boston.

Adams noted that the instinct to revolt against society had become a general tendency among poets after 1850; and he implied that Lodge belonged to the tradition of dissent that had included Byron, Shelley, Swinburne, Verlaine, and Whitman. Then in the deepest irony of a biography informed by irony, Adams concluded that Lodge had acquired an education as antiquated as his own eighteenth-century education. Lodge had failed to recognize that the pose of poet-rebel was obsolete.

Therefore the gap between the poet and the citizen was so wide as to be impassable in Boston, but it was not a division of society into hostile camps, as it had been in England with Shelley and Keats, or in Boston itself, half a century before, with the anti-slavery outbursts of Emerson and Whittier, Longfellow and Lowell, which shook the foundations of the State. The Bostonian of 1900 differed from his parents and grandparents of 1850, in owning nothing the value of which, in the market, could be affected by the poet. Indeed, to him, the poet's pose of hostility to actual conditions of society was itself mercantile,—a form of drama,—a thing to sell, rather than a serious revolt. Society could safely adopt it as a form of industry, as it adopted other forms of bookmaking. (16–17)

By domesticating him, Boston had debilitated the poet and degraded art into merchandise. In short, the poet in 1900 had no audience: "Society was not disposed to defend itself from criticism or attack. Indeed, the most fatal part of the situation for the poet in revolt, the paralyzing drug that made him helpless, was that society no longer seemed sincerely to believe in itself or anything else; it resented nothing, not even praise. The young poet grew up without being able to find an enemy" (17).

Seemingly predestined to failure, Lodge in the biography became depersonalized into a symbol of defeat. Adams's life of Albert Gallatin had attributed Gallatin's political failure to the hostility of random social forces. *The Life of Lodge* became the artistic analogue:

Lodge, like Gallatin or Adams in *The Education*, was doomed by these forces to a series of futile attempts at education. *The Life of Lodge* traced Lodge's steps toward the total failure anticipated from the opening pages. Two months before the publication of *The Life of Lodge*, George Santayana coined a term to describe the cultural conditions Adams felt had stifled Lodge. In "The Genteel Tradition in American Philosophy," Santayana postulated a dialectic in American culture:

America is not simply . . . a young country with an old mentality: it is a country with two mentalities, one a survival of the beliefs and standards of the fathers, the other an expression of the instincts, practice, and discoveries of the younger generation. In all the higher things of the mind—in religion, in literature, in the moral emotions—it is the hereditary spirit that still prevails. . . . That one-half of the American mind, that not occupied intensely in practical affairs, has remained . . . slightly becalmed; it has floated gently in the backwater, while, alongside, in invention and industry and social organization the other half of the mind was leaping down a sort of Niagara Rapids. This division may be found symbolized in American architecture: a neat reproduction of the colonial mansion—with some modern comforts introduced surreptitiously stands beside the sky-scraper. The American Will inhabits the sky-scraper; the American Intellect inhabits the colonial mansion. The one is the sphere of the American man; the other, at least predominantly, of the American woman. The one is all aggressive enterprise; the other is all genteel tradition.[33]

Like the pseudocolonial mansion, "The Genteel Tradition" implied a slavish adherence to intellectual forms whose substance had died. One consequence of "The Genteel Tradition" was the impossibility of poetry: "When a genteel tradition forbids people to confess that they are unhappy, serious poetry and profound religion are closed to them by that; and since human life, in its depths, cannot then express itself openly, imagination is driven for comfort into abstract arts" (51). Santayana considered Whitman to be the only American poet to escape "The Genteel Tradition," but as an alternative Whitman offered only a "self-indulgent" pantheism. American poets seemed obliged either to follow "The Genteel Tradition" or to lapse into Whitman's "poetry of barbarism."

In Santayana's review of Harold Stearns's *Civilization in the United States* (1922), he explicitly acknowledged that the careers of Lodge and his Harvard contemporaries had influenced his conception of "The Genteel Tradition." Similarly in 1936, Santayana explained to William Lyon Phelps the affinity of Oliver Alden in *The Last Puritan* to the Harvard Poets. "An important element in the tragedy of Oliver . . . is drawn from the fate of a whole string of Harvard poets in the 1880's and 1890's—Sanborn, Philip Savage, Hugh McCulloch, Trumbull Stickney, and Cabot Lodge: also Moody. . . . Now all those friends of mine . . . were visibly killed by the lack of air to breathe. . . . The system was deadly, and they hadn't any alternative tradition (as I had) to fall back upon."[34] In Santayana's autobiography, published in the 1940s, he fashioned a crudely literal version of the stifling-atmosphere theory. Speaking of Stickney's death after moving from Europe to America, he concluded: "Still the tumor itself was a sign of maladaptation. The too delicate plant, that had already flowered, couldn't endure the change of soil and temperature, and bred a parasite that choked it."[35]

Santayana's organic metaphors of suffocation and disease clearly influenced the early writings of Van Wyck Brooks, who, like Santayana, has been credited with leading the assault on "The Genteel Tradition." As Douglas Wilson has persuasively argued, Brooks's *America's Coming of Age* (1915) echoed the central thesis of Santayana's 1911 Berkeley address: "The most telling of these points of comparison are found in the initial section, ' "Highbrow" and "Lowbrow." ' . . . There Santayana's notion of the split in the American mind is appropriated by Brooks, modulated, and presented as the key to an understanding of the crisis in American culture."[36]

Brooks's *Literary Life in America* (1921) revealed that he had been influenced by Adams as well as by Santayana. Brooks, without explicit acknowledgment, used *The Life of Lodge* to document the stifling-atmosphere theory:

That there is some truth behind this, that the soil of our society is arid and impoverished, is indicated by the testimony of our own poets. One has only to consider what George Cabot Lodge wrote in 1904 in one of his letters: "We are a dying race, as every race must be of which the men are, as men and not accumulators, third-rate." . . . I go back to the poet Lodge's letters. "Was there ever," he writes, "such an anomaly as the American man? In practical affairs his cynicism, energy and capacity are simply stupefying, and in every other respect he is a sentimental idiot possessing neither the interest, the capacity nor the desire for even the most elementary processes of independent thought. . . ." Is this to be denied?[37]

When Brooks discussed Lodge in *New England: Indian Summer* (1940), he cited both *The Life of Lodge* and Santayana's letter to Phelps to support the contention that "George Cabot Lodge was extinguished in the bottle. He died . . . feeling he had lived in a void."[38]

In Brooks's books of the 1920s, he extended the stifling-atmosphere theory to Twain and to James; and, through his influence and concurrently Vernon L. Parrington's, this idea was widely disseminated. As recently as 1966, Larzer Ziff has argued that the literary generation of the 1890s was "a truly lost generation" that was "cut off before its time" and that absorbed "stunting social shock."[39] That *fin de siècle* American culture inflicted severe psychic damage on its artists and writers has become one of the deeply entrenched orthodoxies of American literary history.

Without question, this idea that found expression in Adams's *Life of Lodge*, Santayana's "Genteel Tradition" speech, and Brooks's early books was a commonplace of educated opinion at the time; and Lodge may well have lived through a traumatic period for literature. However, to argue that Lodge was extinguished by a stifling cultural atmosphere is both to diminish his real, if limited, successes as a writer, and to ignore the familial and personal causes of his literary failures. Because Lodge came to believe in the stifling-atmosphere theory and to use it as an excuse, his failures became in part self-fulfilling prophecies. Thus, the stifling-atmosphere theory is a somewhat circular and necessarily partial explanation of his career. If Lodge was stilled, it was not so much by American culture at large as by what Edith Wharton called "the slightly rarefied atmosphere of mutual admiration, and disdain of the rest of the world," which prevailed in Lodge's Washington circle and which, she claimed, kept Lodge in "a state of brilliant immaturity."[40]

Lodge's elitist and alienated outlook was unquestionably shaped and then reinforced by his father's friends, particularly by Henry Adams and William Sturgis Bigelow; and Lodge eagerly sought their approval. Unable to locate the *avant-garde* of his generation, whose ideas would topple the literary establishment, Lodge joined forces with Adams in what J. C. Levenson has called an *arrière-garde* for literature: "When George Cabot Lodge uttered his second-hand convictions on the degradation of modern society, the failure of the American man, or the need for art to be bad in order to succeed, the Adamsish phrases make the older man seem to have been a corrupter of youth. If there was to have been a school of Henry Adams, it died out because the chief pupil was overwhelmed by the teacher. A weak poet embalms the influences which shape his work; it takes a strong one to keep a tradition alive. How much so may be seen in the case of T. S. Eliot, who, even in his first volume, *Prufrock*, gave a far more vital extension to Adams' achievement than Lodge ever did."[41] It is, of course, obvious that Eliot was a far stronger and more original poet than George Cabot Lodge. But, in fairness to Lodge, it should be added that, if he and his contemporaries failed to escape a poetic genteel tradition, their work anticipated the poetic revolution that was accomplished by Eliot and his generation.

Lodge's achievement was uneven at best. Too often his heightened rhetoric degenerated into bombast, and his vision blurred into abstraction. Even his good poems were marred by technical clumsiness and by Lodge's exasperating preference for vague words rather than concrete images. Nevertheless, in some of his lyrics, sonnets, and blank-verse poems, Lodge's raw rhythmic energy provided an effective vehicle for his passionate celebrations of transcendence and his castigations of the modern age. A few of Lodge's early poems are impressive for their youthful vigor—most notably, "The Song of the Wave," "The East Wind," "Evening," "Youth," "Fall," "Fog at Sea," "The Greek Galley," and "Ishtar." But Lodge's best work is to be found in the disciplined sonnets of *The Great Adventure* (especially in the "Death" section), in the most dramatic parts of *Herakles* (scenes six, seven, and twelve), and in those late poems ("The Noctambulist," "Lower New York," and "Ilion") that evince Lodge's chastened maturity. As a novelist, Lodge has considerable literary-historical interest as a link between the Jamesian and the naturalistic traditions in American fiction; and "The Genius of the Commonplace," now that it has been published, deserves further study.

In short, George Cabot Lodge was a minor author whose limited artistic accomplishments and whose symptomatic career should earn him, if not a high place in the American literary tradition, then at least more recognition than he now enjoys.

Notes and References

Chapter One

1. Henry Cabot Lodge, preface to *Charles Francis Adams, 1835–1915: An Autobiography* (Boston: Houghton Mifflin, 1916), pp. xii–xiii.

2. Quoted by Karl Schriftgiesser in *The Gentleman from Massachusetts: Henry Cabot Lodge* (Boston: Little Brown, 1944), p. 11.

3. Henry Cabot Lodge, *Early Memories* (New York: Scribner's, 1913), p. 13.

4. *The Writings of Oliver Wendell Holmes* (Boston: Houghton Mifflin, 1898), V, 3–4.

5. Cleveland Amory, *The Proper Bostonians*, p. 39.

6. Report card of George Cabot Lodge, Nov. 30, 1888, in George Cabot Lodge Papers.

7. Owen Wister, *Roosevelt: The Story of a Friendship* (New York: Macmillan, 1930), p. 158.

8. Henry Cabot Lodge, *Early Memories*, p. 234.

9. Edith Wharton, *A Backward Glance*, p. 150.

10. Van Wyck Brooks, *Fenollosa and His Circle* (New York: Dutton, 1962), pp. 29–30. Bigelow's "friend" was Margaret T. Chanler; see her *Autumn in the Valley* (Boston: Little Brown, 1936), pp. 23–25.

11. Frederick Cheever Shattuck, "William Sturgis Bigelow," *Proceedings of the Massachusetts Historical Society*, LX (Oct., 1926), 17.

12. Quoted in Henry Adams, *The Life of George Cabot Lodge*, p. 148.

13. Charles Warren Stoddard, "Tuckernuck," *Ave Maria*, LVIII (Jan., 1904), 109, 111.

14. *Poems and Dramas of George Cabot Lodge* (Boston: Houghton Mifflin, 1911), I, 66. All further quotations from Lodge's poems are taken from this edition and are documented in the text.

15. Theodore Roosevelt, *An Autobiography* (1913; rpt. New York: Scribner's, 1920), pp. 93–95.

16. *The Works of Theodore Roosevelt* (New York: Scribner's, 1926), XIII, 319.

17. Letter of Valentine Mitchell Gammell to the author, Nov. 11, 1969.

18. Edith Wharton, "George Cabot Lodge," *Scribner's*, XLVII (Feb., 1910), 236.

19. Adams, *Life of Lodge*, pp. 14, 11–12.

20. Martin Green, *The Problem of Boston*, p. 151.

21. Lewis P. Simpson, *The Man of Letters in New England and the South*, p. 58. Further references are documented in the text.

22. Henry Adams, *The Education of Henry Adams*, pp. 54–55.

23. Norman Hapgood, *The Changing Years* (New York: Farrar & Rinehart, 1930), p. 46.

24. Daniel G. Mason, "At Harvard in the Nineties," *New England Quarterly*, IX (1936), 69.

25. Maurice F. Brown, "Harvard Poetic Renaissance: 1885–1910," p. 2.

26. Lodge to Anna Cabot Lodge [Mar. 7, 1892]. Unless otherwise noted, the texts for all George Cabot Lodge letters are manuscripts in the George Cabot Lodge Papers, Massachusetts Historical Society, Boston. When a letter is quoted that was previously published in Henry Adams's *Life of George Cabot Lodge*, I have so noted. However, in all cases where a manuscript is extant, I have ignored Adams's minor editorial emendations and have quoted the manuscript exactly, preserving Lodge's eccentric punctuation and capitalization. In four instances I have silently corrected Lodge's spelling. Where manuscripts are no longer extant, as in the cases of Lodge's letters to W. S. Bigelow and Marjorie Nott, I have quoted from *The Life of Lodge*. Lodge rarely dated his letters, and some of my dating differs slightly from Adams's.

27. Lodge to Anna Cabot Lodge, May 6, 1893 (*Life of Lodge*, p. 21).

28. Lodge to Anna Cabot Lodge, Dec. 12 [1893] (*Life of Lodge*, p. 22).

29. Lodge to Anna Cabot Lodge [Mar. 31, 1894].

30. Lodge to Anna Cabot Lodge [Mar. 15, 1894] (*Life of Lodge*, pp. 23–24).

31. Lodge to Anna Cabot Lodge [Mar. 19, 1895] (*Life of Lodge*, p. 26).

32. Henry Cabot Lodge, ed., *Selections from the Correspondence of Theodore Roosevelt and Henry Cabot Lodge* (New York: Scribner's, 1925), I, 228, 230.

33. Lodge to Anna Cabot Lodge [May, 1895] (*Life of Lodge*, p. 28).

34. Quoted in Thomas Riggs, "Trumbull Stickney, 1874–1904," p. 56.

35. Arthur Schopenhauer, *The Art of Literature*, trans. T. Bailey Saunders (London: Swan Sonnenschein, 1910), p. 119.

36. Margites Chitterly, "Unimaginary Conversation," *Harvard Monthly*, II (Apr., 1886), 74–78; quoted in Riggs, "Trumbull Stickney," pp. 41–42.

Chapter Two

1. Henry Adams, *The Education of Henry Adams*, p. 80.

2. Lodge to Henry Cabot Lodge [Dec., 1895].

3. Lodge to Anna Cabot Lodge [Dec., 1895]. Lodge thought *The Law of Civilization and Decay* was "horribly true & very well done."

4. Lodge to Henry Cabot Lodge [Dec., 1895].

5. Lodge to Anna Cabot Lodge [Jan. 6, 1896] (*Life of Lodge*, pp. 34–35).

6. Lodge to Henry Cabot Lodge [May 15, 1896].

7. Lodge to Anna Cabot Lodge [Aug., 1896] (*Life of Lodge*, p. 48).

8. Adams, *Education*, p. 77.

9. Lodge to Anna Cabot Lodge [Jan., 1897].

10. From manuscript in George Cabot Lodge Papers.

11. From manuscript in George Cabot Lodge Papers.

12. Lodge to Anna Cabot Lodge, Mar. 22 [1897].

13. Henry Cabot Lodge to Charles Scribner's Sons, Sept. 19, 1898. Charles Scribner's Sons Archives, Princeton University Library.

14. Henry Cabot Lodge, ed., *Selections from the Correspondence of Roosevelt and Lodge* (New York: Scribner's, 1925), I, 378–79.

15. *Nation*, LXVIII (Apr. 27, 1899), 315.

16. *Dial*, XXVI (Jan. 16, 1899), 51.

17. *Harvard Graduates Magazine*, VII (Mar., 1899), 493–94.

18. Howard Mumford Jones, *Guide to American Literature and Its Backgrounds Since 1890*, 2nd ed., rev. (Cambridge: Harvard University Press, 1959), pp. 113–14.

19. Edwin H. Cady, *The Gentleman in America* (Syracuse: Syracuse University Press, 1949), p. 24.

20. Vernon L. Parrington, *The Beginnings of Critical Realism in America* (New York: Harcourt Brace & World, 1958), p. 52.

21. Frederick W. Eckman, "The Language of American Poetry, 1900–1910," p. 4. Further references are documented in the text.

22. F. S, Flint, "Imagisme," *Poetry: A Magazine of Verse*, I (Mar., 1913), 199. See also: Ezra Pound, "Vorticism," *Fortnightly Review*, XCVI (Sep. 1, 1914), 461–71.

23. T. S. Eliot, "Tradition and the Individual Talent," in *Selected Essays* (New York: Harcourt Brace & World, 1958), p. 449.

24. Lodge to Henry Cabot Lodge, Feb. 14 [1896].

25. *Ibid.*

26. Lodge to Anna Cabot Lodge, May 7 [1897].

27. Eckman, "The Language of American Poetry," p. 38.

28. Lodge to Anna Cabot Lodge [Feb., 1897] (*Life of Lodge*, p. 58).

29. Lodge to William Sturgis Bigelow, Dec. 10, 1897 (*Life of Lodge*, pp. 68, 71).

30. Henry Cabot Lodge, ed., *Selections from the Correspondence of Roosevelt and Lodge*, I, 379.

31. Lodge to Anna Cabot Lodge, Mar. 3 [1897].

32. Thomas Riggs, "Trumbull Stickney," p. 111.

33. Larzer Ziff, *The American 1890s*, p. 313.

34. Lodge to Anna Cabot Lodge [Jan., 1897] (*Life of Lodge*, p. 52).

35. Lodge to Anna Cabot Lodge [Feb., 1897] (*Life of Lodge*, pp. 58–59).

36. Henry Adams, *Life of Lodge*, pp. 83–84, 15–16.

37. Edith Wharton, *A Backward Glance*, p. 150.

38. Charles Henry Davis to Henry Cabot Lodge, July 20, 1898 (*Life of Lodge*, p. 82).

39. Lodge to Henry Cabot Lodge [Aug., 1898] (*Life of Lodge*, p. 77).

40. Lodge to Henry Cabot Lodge, Aug. 10, 1898 (*Life of Lodge*, pp. 81–82).

41. Lodge to Beatrice Demarest Lloyd [Feb., 1900]. E. C. Stedman Collection, Columbia University Library.

42. Lodge to Anna Cabot Lodge, Aug. 12 [1899].

43. Lodge to Anna Cabot Lodge [July, 1899] (*Life of Lodge*, pp. 89–90).

44. Lodge to Anna Cabot Lodge [Mar., 1900].

45. Lodge to Bigelow, Dec. 24, 1901.

46. Edward Burlingame to Henry Cabot Lodge, Jan. 23, 1902. Henry Cabot Lodge Papers, Massachusetts Historical Society. Printed with permission of Charles Scribner's Sons.

47. Lodge to Anna Cabot Lodge [?Oct., 1902].

Chapter Three

1. Henry Adams, *The Education of Henry Adams*, pp. 405–06.

2. Henry Adams to Lodge, Feb. 16, 1897 (letter in possession of Henry Cabot Lodge).

3. Adams, *Education*, p. 406.

4. J. C. Levenson, *The Mind and Art of Henry Adams*, p. 296.

5. From the typescript of the novel in George Cabot Lodge Papers, p. 27. All further references are documented in the text.

6. Lodge, *The Great Adventure*, p. 23.

7. From Lodge's manuscript outline of an essay on Conservative Christian Anarchism in George Cabot Lodge Papers. I have borrowed phrases from this outline elsewhere in my discussion.

8. Michael Wreszin, "Albert Jay Nock and the Anarchist Elitist Tradition in America," *American Quarterly*, XXI (1969), 166–67. Lodge's ideas also closely resemble those of the "Anarchist" in G. Lowes Dickinson's influential *A Modern Symposium* (New York: McClure Phillips, 1905). The "Anarchist," who claims William Blake, P. B. Shelley, and Jesus as allies, defines his philosophy: "To shatter material bonds that we may bind the closer the bonds of the soul, to slough dead husks that we may liberate living forms, to abolish institutions that we may evoke energies, to put off the material and put on the spiritual body, that, whether we fight with the tongue or the sword, is the inspiration of our movement, that, and that only, is the true and inner meaning of anarchy" (58).

9. Lodge to Anna Cabot Lodge [Dec., 1900].

10. Lodge, "The Genius of the Commonplace," in *George Cabot Lodge: Selected Fiction and Verse*, ed. John W. Crowley, p. 4. Further references are documented in the text.

11. Lodge to Adams [Sept., 1900]. Henry Adams Papers, Massachusetts Historical Society.

12. Adams to Lodge, Apr. 22, 1903; in *Henry Adams and His Friends*, ed. Harold Dean Cater, pp. 542–43. Cater erroneously assumed that Adams was referring in this letter to the manuscript of *Cain*.

13. Lodge to Adams [Apr., 1903]. Henry Adams Papers.

14. From Lodge's copy of Walt Whitman's *Leaves of Grass* (Boston: Small Maynard, 1899) in George Cabot Lodge Papers.

15. From manuscript of "Servae Laudes" in George Cabot Lodge Papers.

16. *Harvard Graduates Magazine*, XI (Mar., 1903), 475.

17. Frederick W. Conner, *Cosmic Optimism*, p. 307.

Chapter Four

1. Lodge, "The Genius of the Commonplace," in *George Cabot Lodge: Selected Fiction and Verse*; p. 108.

2. Henry Adams, *Life of Lodge*, pp. 109–10.

3. Henry Adams to Lodge, Dec. 1, 1904 (letter in possession of Henry Cabot Lodge).

4. *Dial*, XXXVIII (Jan. 16, 1905), 48.

5. *Nation*, LXXX (Jan. 26, 1905), 73.

6. *Independent*, LVIII (Apr. 6, 1905), 783–84.

7. *Harvard Graduates Magazine*, XIII (Mar., 1905), 548.

8. Maurice F. Brown, "Harvard Poetic Renaissance," pp. 321, 307.

9. *Ibid.*, pp. 311–12.

10. Jay Martin, *Harvests of Change* (Englewood Cliffs, N.J.: Prentice Hall, 1967), pp. 87–88.

11. Thomas Riggs, "Prometheus 1900," *American Literature*, XXII (Jan., 1951), 421.

12. Margaret T. Chanler, *Roman Spring*, p. 292.

13. Adams to Charles Warren Stoddard, Dec. 20, 1904. Henry Adams Papers, Massachusetts Historical Society.

14. Lodge to Anna Cabot Lodge [Sept., 1898].

15. *Nation*, LXXVI (Mar. 12, 1903), 214.

16. Lodge to Elizabeth Lodge, Aug., 1904 (*Life of Lodge*, p. 120).

17. Lodge to Elizabeth Lodge, Sept. 1, 1904 (*Life of Lodge*, p. 121).

18. Lodge to Anna Cabot Lodge [June, 1905](*Life of Lodge*, p. 139).

19. Adams, *Life of Lodge*, p. 141.

20. *Century*, LXXI (Nov., 1905), 156.

21. *Dial*, XL (Feb. 16, 1906), 126.

22. *Nation*, LXXXI (Dec. 21, 1905), 507–08.

23. *North American Review*, CLXXXII (May, 1906), 759–60.
24. *Harvard Graduates Magazine*, XIV (June, 1906), 741.
25. William Vaughn Moody to Lodge, Mar. 31, 1905. George Cabot Lodge Papers, Massachusetts Historical Society.
26. Moody to Lodge, Feb. 19, 1905. George Cabot Lodge Papers.
27. From page proofs in George Cabot Lodge Papers, p. xxiv.
28. Moody to Lodge, July 25, 1905. George Cabot Lodge Papers.
29. Moody to Lodge, Aug. 19, 1905. George Cabot Lodge Papers.
30. Moody to Lodge, Nov. 26, 1906. George Cabot Lodge Papers.

Chapter Five

1. Henry Adams to Lodge, Nov. 10, 1905 (letter in possession of Henry Cabot Lodge).
2. Lodge to Langdon Mitchell [Sept., 1905].
3. Lodge to Mitchell [?Spring, 1906].
4. Lodge to Mitchell [Spring, 1904] (*Life of Lodge*, p. 128).
5. Lodge to Mitchell [Spring, 1906] (*Life of Lodge*, pp. 189–90).
6. *Ibid.* (*Life of Lodge*, p. 191).
7. Mrs. Winthrop Gray to Mrs. Davis, July, 1906 (letter in possession of Henry Cabot Lodge).
8. Edith Wharton to Sara Norton, July 7, 1906. Edith Wharton Papers, Collection of American Literature, Yale University Library. Printed with permission.
9. Lodge to Anna Cabot Lodge [Oct., 1906].
10. Henry Adams, *Life of Lodge*, p. 157.
11. *Ibid.*, p. 145.
12. Lodge to Marjorie Nott, Sept. 30, 1907 (*Life of Lodge*, pp. 183–84).
13. Lodge to Mitchell [Autumn, 1907].
14. This is the opinion of Dr. George Cheever Shattuck, recognized authority on tropical diseases, expressed in a letter to the author, Aug. 30, 1969. Dr. Shattuck (b. 1879) as a youth often went to Tuckernuck Island and once met Lodge there.
15. Adams, *Life of Lodge*, p. 162.
16. F. A. Robinson to Henry Cabot Lodge, May 22, 1916, quoted in John W. Crowley, "E. A. Robinson and Henry Cabot Lodge," *New England Quarterly*, XLIII (1970), 117.
17. Frederick W. Conner, *Cosmic Optimism*, p. 313.

Chapter Six

1. Alfred Kazin, "History and Henry Adams," *New York Review of Books*, XIII (Oct. 23, 1969), 25, 29.
2. Lodge to Marjorie Nott, Dec. 17, 1908 (*Life of Lodge*, p. 187).
3. R. C. Trevelyan to Bernard Berenson, Mar. 10, 1909. Henry Adams Papers, Massachusetts Historical Society.

4. Henry Adams to Lodge, Mar. 11, 1909 (Cater, *Henry Adams and His Friends*, p. 644n).

5. Adams to Lodge, Dec. 2, 1908 (Cater, p. 629).

6. Brooks Adams to Lodge, Dec. 25, 1908, George Cabot Lodge Papers, Massachusetts Historical Society.

7. S. Weir Mitchell to Lodge, Nov. 30, 1908. George Cabot Lodge Papers.

8. Edith Wharton to Lodge, Dec. 26, 1908. George Cabot Lodge Papers.

9. Henry James to Lodge, Dec. 12, 1908. George Cabot Lodge Papers.

10. *Harvard Graduates Magazine*, XVII (Mar., 1909), 563.

11. *New York Times Book Review*, XIII (Dec. 26, 1908), 801.

12. *Dial*, XLVII (Aug. 1, 1909), 69–70.

13. Alfred H. Brown to Lodge, Jan. 4, 1909. George Cabot Lodge Papers.

14. Adams to Lodge [Jan. 8, 1909] (Cater, p. 643n).

15. Lodge to Adams, July 16, 1909. Henry Adams Papers.

16. *Ibid.*

17. Lodge to Nott, July 8, 1909. Henry Adams Papers.

18. Lodge to Anna Cabot Lodge [July, 1909] (*Life of Lodge*, p. 201).

19. William Wordsworth, "Composed Upon Westminster Bridge, Sept. 3, 1802" in *English Romantic Poetry*, ed. Harold Bloom (New York: Anchor, 1963),pp. 307–08.

20. Monroe K. Spears, *Dionysus and the City* (New York: Oxford University Press, 1971), p. 71.

21. Lodge to Anna Cabot Lodge, [July 21, 1909].

22. Lodge to W. S. Bigelow, Aug. 18, 1909 (*Life of Lodge*, pp. 205 06).

23. Quoted in a letter from Brown to Henry Cabot Lodge, Aug. 23, 1909. Henry Cabot Lodge Papers, Massachusetts Historical Society.

24. Elizabeth Cameron to Anna Cabot Lodge, Sept. 25 [1909]. George Cabot Lodge Papers.

25. [Frank Colby to Edith Wharton, July, 1910]; quoted in Henry Adams, *Life of Lodge*, pp. 142–43.

Chapter Seven

1. Henry Cabot Lodge to Bigelow, Sept. 5, 1909. Henry Cabot Lodge Papers, Massachusetts Historical Society.

2. See: Henry Cabot Lodge to Corinne Roosevelt Robinson, Sept. 3, 1909 (Houghton Library); Henry Cabot Lodge to Adams, Sept. 16, 1909 (Henry Adams Papers); Henry Cabot Lodge to Wharton, Sept. 28, 1909 (Edith Wharton Papers).

3. Edith Wharton, "George Cabot Lodge," 236, 238.

4. Alfred H. Brown, "The Poetry of George Cabot Lodge," *Twentieth Century Magazine*, I (1910), 403.

5. Theodore Roosevelt, "Introduction," *Poems and Dramas of George Cabot Lodge*, I, xiii, vi.

6. Henry Adams to Elizabeth Cameron, Jan. 24, 1910; in *Letters of Henry Adams (1892–1918)*, ed. Worthington C. Ford (Boston: Houghton Mifflin, 1938), p. 531.

7. Adams to Cameron, May 29, 1910 (Ford, p. 543).

8. Anna Cabot Lodge to Adams, [Oct., 1910]. George Cabot Lodge Papers, Massachusetts Historical Society.

9. Adams to Elizabeth Lodge, Oct. 24, 1910 (letter in possession of Henry Cabot Lodge).

10. Adams to Elizabeth Lodge, May 3, 1910 (letter in possession of Henry Cabot Lodge).

11. Adams to Elizabeth Lodge, July 29, 1910 (letter in possession of Henry Cabot Lodge).

12. Edmund Wilson, *The Shock of Recognition*, p. 744.

13. Adams to Elizabeth Lodge, Oct. 25, 1911 (letter in possession of Henry Cabot Lodge).

14. Adams to Elizabeth Lodge, June 16, 1910 (letter in possession of Henry Cabot Lodge).

15. Adams to Cameron, Feb. 7, 1911 (Ford, pp. 560–61).

16. Adams to Houghton Mifflin Company, Apr., 1911. Henry Cabot Lodge Papers.

17. Adams to Cameron, Apr. 16, 1911 (Ford, p. 566n).

18. *Dial*, LII (Jan. 1, 1912), 27.

19. *Nation*, XCIV (May 30, 1912), 538.

20. *Literary Digest*, XLIII (Dec. 30, 1911), 1236.

21. *Independent*, LXXI (Nov. 16, 1911), 1083–84.

22. *New York Times Review of Books*, XVII (Mar. 24, 1912), 161.

23. P. C. Pavolini, "George Cabot Lodge," *Living Age*, 7th ser., LIX (May 17, 1913), 400, 408.

24. James Gibbons Huneker to Henry Cabot Lodge, Oct. 31, 1915; in *Letters of James Gibbons Huneker*, ed. Josephine Huneker p. 200.

25. James G. Huneker, *Steeplejack*, II, 209–10.

26. Robinson to Henry Cabot Lodge, May 22, 1916; quoted in Crowley, "E. A. Robinson and Henry Cabot Lodge," 117.

27. Van Wyck Brooks, *New England: Indian Summer*, pp. 457–58.

28. Horace Gregory and Marya Zaturenska, *A History of American Poetry, 1900–1940*, pp. 28–32.

29. Louise Bogan, *Achievement in American Poetry*, p. 28.

30. E. C. Stedman, *An American Anthology, 1787–1899* (Boston: Houghton Mifflin, 1900), p. xxviii.

31. George Hochfield, *Henry Adams: An Introduction and Interpretation* (New York: Barnes & Noble, 1962), p. 142.

32. Henry Adams, *Life of Lodge*, p. 6. All further references are documented in the text.

33. George Santayana, "The Genteel Tradition in American Philosophy" (1911), rpt. in *The Genteel Tradition*, ed. Douglas L. Wilson, pp. 39–40.

34. *The Letters of George Santayana*, ed. Daniel Cory (New York: Scribner's, 1955), p. 306.

35. George Santayana, *The Middle Span* (New York: Scribner's 1945), p. 150.

36. Wilson, ed., *The Genteel Tradition*, pp. 20–21.

37. Van Wyck Brooks, *Three Essays on America* (New York: Dutton, 1970), pp. 199–201.

38. Brooks, *New England: Indian Summer*, p. 457.

39. Larzer Ziff, *The American 1890s*, p. 348.

40. Edith Wharton, *A Backward Glance*, p. 151.

41. J. C. Levenson, *The Mind and Art of Henry Adams*, pp. 379, 386.

Selected Bibliography

PRIMARY SOURCES

1. Manuscript Collections

Beverly, Massachusetts. George Cabot Lodge Papers, in possession of Henry Cabot Lodge.
Boston. Massachusetts Historical Society. George Cabot Lodge Papers.
Boston. Massachusetts Historical Society. Henry Cabot Lodge Papers.
Boston. Massachusetts Historical Society. Henry Adams Papers.
Cambridge. Harvard University Archives.
Cambridge. Harvard University. Relevant collections in Houghton Library.
New Haven. Yale University Library. Edith Wharton Papers.
New York. American Academy of Arts and Letters Archives.
New York. Columbia University Library. E. C. Stedman Collection.
New York. New York Public Library. The Century Collection.
Princeton. Princeton University Library, Charles Scribner's Sons Archives.

2. Poems in Magazines

"Sonnet." Harvard Monthly, XX (May, 1895), 117.
"Sonnet." Scribner's, XIX (Apr., 1896), 500.
"Tuckanuck." Harper's, XCIII (July, 1896), 285.
"After." Scribner's, XX (Aug., 1896), 178.
"A Song of the Wave." Scribner's, XXI (June, 1897), 707–08.
"The Greek Galley." Scribner's, XXIX (Feb., 1901), 185–86.
"Outward!." Scribner's, XXX (Aug., 1901), 177.
"The Passage." Atlantic Monthly, LXXXIX (Jan., 1902), 74–75.
"Vista." Century, LXV (Dec., 1902), 186–87.
"Faith." Scribner's, XXXIV (Oct., 1903), 480.
"Odysseus." Scribner's, XXXVI (July, 1904), 97.
"Primavera." Scribner's, XXXVI (Dec., 1904), 696.
"Trumbull Stickney." Harvard Monthly, XL (May, 1905), 111.
"Moriturus." Scribner's, XXXVIII (July, 1905), 42.
"To Night." Century, LXXI (Nov., 1905), 156.
"Lower New York." Atlantic Monthly, XCVII (Mar., 1906), 339.

"By Day and Night." *Scribner's,* XXXIX (Apr., 1906), 454.
"The Soul's Inheritance." *Scribner's,* XL (Sept., 1906), 362–65.
"The Sleeper." *Scribner's,* XLI (Feb., 1907), 166.
"Interpretations." *Scribner's,* XLI (Apr., 1907), 505.
"Ventures and Consummations." *Scribner's,* XLII (Oct., 1907), 477.
"Cor Cordium." *Scribner's,* XLVI (July, 1909), 27.
"Ilion." *Scribner's,* XLVI (Nov., 1909), 607.

3. Books
The Song of the Wave and Other Poems. New York: Scribner's, 1898.
Poems (1899–1902). New York: Cameron & Blake, 1902.
Cain: A Drama. Boston: Houghton Mifflin, 1904.
The Great Adventure. Boston: Houghton Mifflin, 1905.
The Poems of Trumbull Stickney. Boston: Houghton Mifflin, 1905. Coeditor
    with John Ellerton Lodge and William Vaughn Moody.
Herakles. Boston: Houghton Mifflin, 1908.
The Soul's Inheritance and Other Poems. Boston: Houghton Mifflin, 1909.
Poems and Dramas of George Cabot Lodge. 2 vols. Boston: Houghton
    Mifflin, 1911.
Poems and Dramas of George Cabot Lodge. 2 vols. London: Heinemann,
    1912.

4. Reprints
The Song of the Wave and Other Poems. Upper Saddle River, N.J.: Gregg
    Press, 1970.
George Cabot Lodge: Selected Fiction and Verse. Ed. John W. Crowley. St.
    Paul: John Colet Press, 1976.

SECONDARY SOURCES

ADAMS, HENRY. *The Education of Henry Adams.* Boston: Houghton
    Mifflin, 1918. See pages 403–08 for background of Conservative Christ-
    ian Anarchism.
————. *The Life of George Cabot Lodge.* Boston: Houghton Miffln, 1911.
    Brilliant and indispensable study.
————. *Henry Adams and His Friends.* Ed. Harold Dean Cater. Boston:
    Houghton Mifflin, 1947. Contains several letters from Adams to
    Lodge.
AMORY, CLEVELAND. *The Proper Bostonians.* New York: Dutton, 1947.
    Helpful about Lodge's family background.
BOGAN, LOUISE. *Achievement in American Poetry, 1900–1950.* Chicago:
    Regnery, 1951. Brief discussion of Lodge.

BROOKS, VAN WYCK. *New England: Indian Summer, 1865–1915*. New York: Dutton, 1940. Brief, unsympathetic treatment.

BROWN, ALFRED H. "The Poetry of George Cabot Lodge." *Twentieth Century Magazine*, I (1910), 403–14. Enthusiastic essay by a Lodge disciple.

BROWN, MAURICE F. "Harvard Poetic Renaissance: 1885–1910." Doctoral dissertation, Harvard University, 1958. Excellent study of the Harvard Poets and their intellectual backgrounds.

CHANLER, MARGARET TERRY. *Roman Spring*. Boston: Little Brown, 1935. Perceptive remembrance of Lodge.

CHISOLM, LAWRENCE W. *Fenollosa: The Far East and American Culture*. New Haven: Yale University Press, 1963. Discusses Lodge's interest in Buddhism and his friendship with W. S. Bigelow.

CONNER, FREDERICK W. *Cosmic Optimism*. Gainesville: University of Florida Press, 1949. Places Lodge in the tradition of American Transcendentalism.

CROWLEY, JOHN W. "The Education of George Cabot Lodge: A Literary Biography." Doctoral dissertation, Indiana University, 1970. Fullest biography.

———. "E. A. Robinson and Henry Cabot Lodge." *New England Quarterly*, XLIII (1970), 115–24. Quotes Robinson's favorable reaction to *Poems and Dramas*.

———. "George Gissing and George Cabot Lodge." *Gissing Newsletter*, VI (1970), 7–9. Documents their friendship.

———. "'Dear Bay': Theodore Roosevelt's Letters to George Cabot Lodge." *New York History*, LIII (1972), 177–94.

———. "Eden Off Nantucket: W. S. Bigelow and 'Tuckanuck.'" *Essex Institute Historical Collections*, CIX (1973), 3–8

———. "George Cabot Lodge (1873–1909)." *American Literary Realism*, VI (1973), 44–50. Review of Lodge research.

———. "The Suicide of the Artist: Henry Adams' *Life of George Cabot Lodge*." *New England Quarterly*, XLVI (1973), 189–204. Places *Life of Lodge* in context of Adams's late writings.

———. "Whitman and the Harvard Poets: The Case of George Cabot Lodge." *Walt Whitman Review*, XIX (1973), 165–68. Discusses Lodge's admiration for Whitman.

ECKMAN, FREDERICK W. "The Language of American Poetry, 1900–1910." Doctoral dissertation, Ohio State University, 1954. Excellent study of Lodge and others.

FLANDRAU, CHARLES MACOMB. "George Cabot Lodge." In *Harvard College Class of 'Ninety-five: Fourth Report*. Cambridge: Harvard University Press, 1910. Brief biographical sketch.

GARRATY, JOHN A. *Henry Cabot Lodge: A Biography*. New York: Knopf, 1953. Useful background source.

GREEN, MARTIN. *The Problem of Boston.* New York: Norton, 1966. Persuasive study of Boston's cultural decay in the nineteenth century.

G[REENSLET], F[ERRIS]. "George Cabot Lodge." In *Dictionary of American Biography.* New York: Scribner's, 1943.

GREGORY, HORACE, and MARYA ZATURENSKA. *A History of American Poetry, 1900–1940.* New York: Harcourt Brace, [1946]. Hostile to Lodge.

HALDANE, SEÁN. *The Fright of Time: Joseph Trumbull Stickney 1874–1904.* Ladysmith, Quebec: Ladysmith Press, 1970. Quotes several Lodge letters; documents his friendship with Stickney.

HATCH, ALDEN. *The Lodges of Massachusetts.* New York: Hawthorn Books, 1973. Superficial chapter on Lodge.

HUNEKER, JAMES GIBBONS. *Steeplejack.* 2 vols. New York: Scribner's, 1920. Includes reminiscence of Lodge in Paris.

———. *Letters of James Gibbons Huneker.* Ed. Josephine Huneker. New York: Scribner's, 1922. Contains Huneker's warm response to *Poems and Dramas.*

JONES, HOWARD MUMFORD. *The Bright Medusa.* Urbana: University of Illinois Press, 1952. Important assessment of the Harvard Poets.

———. *The Age of Energy: Varieties of American Experience, 1865–1915.* New York: Viking, 1971. Excellent chapter on "The Genteel Tradition"; brief discussion of Lodge.

KINDILIEN, CARLIN T. *American Poetry in the Eighteen-Nineties.* Providence: Brown University Press, 1956. Discusses *The Song of the Wave.*

LEVENSON, J. C. *The Mind and Art of Henry Adams.* Boston: Houghton Mifflin, 1957. Excellent discussion of Lodge's relationship with Adams.

LEWIS, R. W. B. *Edith Wharton: A Biography.* New York: Harper & Row, 1975. Touches on Wharton's friendship with Lodge.

MACKAYE, PERCY. "George Cabot Lodge, '95." *Harvard Graduates Magazine,* XVIII (1909), 243–45. Brief obituary.

[MACY, JOHN A.]. "The State of Pseudo-Poetry at the Present Time." *Bookman,* XXVII (1908), 513–17. Includes "Unrequited Intuitions," a good parody of Lodge's sonnets.

MILLER, WILLIAM J. *Henry Cabot Lodge [Jr.]: A Biography.* New York: Heineman, 1967. Useful background source.

PAVOLINI, P. C. "George Cabot Lodge." *Living Age,* 7th ser., LIX (May 17, 1913), 400–408. Favorable early study; focus on *Herakles.*

RIGGS, THOMAS. "Trumbull Stickney, 1874–1904." Doctoral dissertation, Princeton University, 1949. Quotes Lodge letters; discusses perceptively *The Song of the Wave.*

———. "Prometheus 1900." *American Literature,* XXII (January, 1951), 399–423. Includes good study of Lodge's verse-dramas.

ROOSEVELT, THEODORE. "Introduction" to *Poems and Dramas of George Cabot Lodge*. Boston: Houghton Mifflin, 1911. Adulatory essay.

SAMUELS, ERNEST, *Henry Adams: The Major Phase*. Cambridge: Harvard University Press, 1964. Discusses Lodge's work and his relationship with Adams.

SANTAYANA, GEORGE. *The Genteel Tradition*. Ed. Douglas L. Wilson. Cambridge: Harvard University Press, 1967. Collection of Santayana's pronouncements on this subject; contains several references to Lodge.

SIMPSON, LEWIS P. *The Man of Letters in New England and the South*. Baton Rouge: Louisiana State University Press, 1973. First four chapters provide excellent background material.

WHARTON, EDITH. "George Cabot Lodge." *Scribner's Magazine*, XLVII (1910), 236–39. Warm and perceptive early study.

―――. *A Backward Glance*. New York: Appleton Century, 1934. Recalls Lodge as pathetic victim of his family circle.

WILSON, EDMUND. "Introduction" to reprint of *Life of Lodge* in *The Shock of Recognition*. New York: Modern Library, n.d. Sees Adams as being bitterly ironic toward Lodge.

ZIFF, LARZER. *The American 1890s*. New York: Viking, 1966. Intelligent but unsympathetic discussion of Lodge.

Index